WHAT DO YOU THINK OF THE PRIEST?

WHAT DO YOU THINK OF THE PRIEST?

A Bibliography on
the Catholic Priesthood

Compiled and Edited by
The Reverend Theophil T. Mierzwinski

WITH A FOREWORD BY
THE MOST REVEREND JOHN F. WHEALON,
ARCHBISHOP OF HARTFORD

An Exposition-University Book
EXPOSITION PRESS   NEW YORK

EXPOSITION PRESS, INC.

50 Jericho Turnpike, Jericho, New York 11753

FIRST EDITION

© 1972 by Theophil T. Mierzwinski. All rights reserved, including the right of reproduction in whole or in part in any form except for short quotations in critical essays and reviews. Manufactured in the United States of America.

LIBRARY OF CONGRESS CATALOG CARD NUMBER: 72-86589

SBN 0-682-47527-0

"Per Mariam ad Jesum in Spiritu Sancto;
Per Jesum ad Patrem in Spiritu Sancto."

To
FATHER JAMES CONEFREY
for
Twenty-five years of
direction and friendship

Contents

	FOREWORD *by the* MOST REVEREND JOHN F. WHEALON	11
	PREFACE	13
1	PRIESTS IN LITERATURE	19
2	PRIEST-SAINTS: BIOGRAPHIES	25
3	PRIESTS: BIOGRAPHIES	31
4	THE PRIESTHOOD	41
	Writings Prior to Vatican Council II	41
	Writings During and After Vatican Council II (1962–1965)	46
5	THE PRIESTHOOD IN PAPAL DOCUMENTS	51
	Major Documents—Twentieth Century	51
	Abbreviations of Magazines Cited	53
	Other Papal Documents	60
	Pius XII (1939–1958)	60
	John XXIII (1958–1963)	64
	Paul VI (1963–)	69
6	THE POPE AND VATICAN COUNCIL II	77
	Fathers of Vatican Council II	78
	American Bishops	80
	The Third Synod of Bishops	81
	EPILOGUE	83
	A PRAYER FOR VOCATIONS TO THE PRIESTHOOD	85
	INDEX OF AUTHORS	87
	INDEX OF SUBJECTS	93

Foreword

In October, 1971, the Third Synod of Bishops in Rome discussed at length the ministerial priesthood in the post-Vatican II world. In that timely discussion the bishops actually continued other earlier studies on the priesthood—massive studies commissioned by the United States Bishops and by other hierarchies; the Decree on Priestly Life and Ministry of Vatican II; the famous papal encyclicals on the priesthood; writings of doctors and saints of the Church; and the New Testament itself.

As a seminarian and later as a seminary rector I used to read and reread these earlier presentations of priestly ideals. They strongly influenced my own priestly vocation. Now, over a quarter century after ordination I try to face all recurring challenges with the consoling knowledge that those who went before in the history of priesthood had many greater challenges to face—and left behind a clear record of ideals to follow for priestly life today.

Father Theophil Mierzwinski, librarian of St. Thomas Seminary of the Archdiocese of Hartford, has painstakingly compiled this bibliographic commentary on the Catholic Priesthood. For this useful instrument I warmly commend Father Mierzwinski. With him I pray that the highest priestly ideals expressed by these books will be lived out existentially by priests old and young, of today and of generations yet to come.

May 26, 1972　　　　　　　MOST REVEREND JOHN F. WHEALON
　　　　　　　　　　　　　　　Archbishop of Hartford

Preface

The theme of this bibliographic work derives from the following excerpt of the words addressed to a general audience by Pope Paul VI, on October 13, 1971:

... And this is enough to justify our question: What do you think of the priest?

We think we are not wrong in assuming that, surprised by the question, you see in your imagination two series of figures of the priest. In the first place, there are the figures of literary reminiscences. Literature has presented us with a gallery of images which are somehow impressed on our memories: ridiculous images and solemn images, caricatures and saints. The priest is a character that lends himself to the writer who is more interested in the characters on the stage than in the stage itself, that is, the facts narrated. He is a character full of hidden aspects, which force a comparison between the exterior reality of the priest and the interior reality that he should possess; he is a figure on two levels. "In me," Leo Trese writes, "there is something of the lion and something of the lamb; there is charity and selfishness; penance and love of comfort; prayers and profanity; humility and pride." (*Vessel of Clay*, p. 139). As St. Paul wrote of himself: "We have this treasure (the Gospel) in earthen vessels, to show that the transcendent power belongs to God and not to us." (2 Cor. 4:7)

Now literature has taken pleasure in depicting this paradoxical dualism in so many different ways that it makes it difficult for the reader to choose the type of priest he prefers, to condemn him, or to mock him or to admire him, or to understand him in his inner self; (for example, think of the figures of ecclesiastics in such well-known authors as Manzoni, Fogazzaro, Marino Moretti, Barbey d'Aurevilly, Chesterton, Bernanos, Cronin, Graham Greene, Marshall, etc).

But then there comes the second series, also very varied, the series of priests that have really existed: the saints such as St. Vincent de Paul, Don Bosco, the Cure d'Ars and let us add Maximilian Kolbe (whom we will declare Blessed on Sunday). And alongside these great figures (and there are thousands of them) there are other dear and modest images of good, holy priests, that each of us, we suppose, has met along his own path: parish priests, religious, teachers, assistants, chaplains . . . They have added to the specifically ministerial charismatic gift of the Word of God and of sacramental Grace something of their own, their own humble, human way of inviting, welcoming, listening, admonishing, sympathizing, consoling, understanding, doing good, . . . and then a style of life of their own, poor and strong, which has made us drop our head thoughtfully, saying to ourselves: yes, this is a real priest. (*L'Osservatore Romano*, English edition, no. 42 [186], pp. 1, 12 October 21, 1971.)

The pastoral musings of Pope Paul VI provided the immediate spur for this bibliography on the Catholic priest and the priesthood. At the time, the Third Synod of Bishops was in the midst of its deliberations on the ministerial priesthood.

The Pope's words supply a framework of generic annotations for the books listed in each section. These, in turn, represent the compiler's bibliographical commentary on Pope Paul's text. Most of the titles are concrete realities on the shelves of the Saint Thomas Seminary Library. Hopefully, the bibliography can be of service to young men of high school and college years, to theological students, and to the ordained clergy.

The compiler decided to include a section listing papal utterances on the priesthood. In conjunction with these, other documents from the Second Vatican Council, the American bishops, and the Third Synod of Bishops are also cited. These references contribute to the value of the compilation as a source book on the Catholic priesthood.

Preface

The titles have been checked for accuracy with the superb indexing of the *Guide to Catholic Literature* (1888–1967), the *Catholic Periodical Index* (1930–1967), and the *Catholic Periodical and Literature Index* (1967–1971). These publications of the Catholic Library Association supplied the bibliographical data of entries that are not found in the Saint Thomas Seminary Library collection.

In the separate lists are found many-faceted responses from a multitude of authors, principally of the twentieth century, to the question of Pope Paul. "What do you think of the Priest?" Brought together in a single bibliographic commentary, they reveal, it is hoped, an answer still in process of formulation by the compiler, who is both a priest and a librarian.

THEOPHIL T. MIERZWINSKI

May 6, 1972

WHAT DO YOU THINK OF THE PRIEST?

1 Priests in Literature

". . . In the first place, there are the figures of literary reminiscences. Literature has presented us with a gallery of images which are somehow impressed on our memories: ridiculous images and solemn images, caricatures and saints . . ."

N.B. Titles marked with an asterisk (*) may be of special interest to teen-agers.

Bazin, R. *Magnificat*. Macmillan, 1932.
*Belair, R. *The Road Less Traveled*. Doubleday, 1964.
Bernanos, G. *The Diary of a County Priest*. Macmillan, 1964.
―――――. *The Star of Satan*. Macmillan, 1940.
Bordeaux, H. *A Pathway to Heaven*. Pellegrini & Cudahy, 1952.
*Brady, L. *Edge of Doom*. Dutton, 1949.

Caldwell, T. *Grandmother and the Priest*. Doubleday, 1963.
*Cather, W. *Death Comes for the Archbishop*. Knopf, 1927.
*Cesbron, G. *Saints in Hell*. Doubleday, 1954.
*Chesterton, G. K. *Father Brown Omnibus*. Dodd, 1945.
*Coccioli, Carlo. *Heaven and Earth*. Prentice-Hall, 1952.
Cooper, E. *No Little Thing*. Doubleday, 1960.
*Cronin, A. J. *Keys of the Kingdom*. Little, Brown, 1941.
Cunningham, M. *The Bishop Finds a Way*. Farrar, Straus & Young, 1955.

*Dever, J. *Three Priests*. Doubleday, 1958.
*Dewohl, Louis. *Citadel of God: A Novel of St. Benedict*. Lippincott, 1959.
* ―――――. *The Glorious Folly: A Novel of the Time of St. Paul*. Lippincott, 1957.
* ―――――. *The Golden Thread:* About St. Ignatius. Lippincott, 1952.
* ―――――. *The Quiet Light: A Novel of St. Thomas Aquinas*. Lippincott, 1950.
* ―――――. *The Restless Flame:* About St. Augustine. Lippincott, 1951.
* ―――――. *Set All Afire: A Novel of St. Francis Xavier*. Lippincott, 1953.

Priests in Literature

*Doty, William. *Fire in the Rain*. Bruce, 1951.
*⎯⎯⎯⎯. *The Mark*. Bruce, 1953.
*⎯⎯⎯⎯. *The Rise of Father Roland*. Bruce, 1961.
*Dudley, O. F. *The Masterful Monk*. Longmans. 1935.
⎯⎯⎯⎯. *Tremaynes and the Masterful Monk*. Longmans, 1940.

*Edwards, Edward. *The Chosen*. Longmans, Green, 1949.
*⎯⎯⎯⎯. *These Two Hands*. Bruce, 1942.
*⎯⎯⎯⎯. *Thy People, My People*. Bruce, 1941.
Englebert, O. *The Wisdom of Father Pecquet*. McKay, 1951.

Faherty, W. *A Wall of San Sebastian*. Academy Guild Press, 1962.

Gironella, J. M. *Cypresses Believe in God*. Knopf, 1955.
*Godden, Rumer. *An Episode of Sparrows: A novel*. Viking, 1955.
Goudge, E. *Gentian Hill*. Coward-McCann, 1949.
*Greene, Graham. *The Power and the Glory*. Viking, 1946.
*Guareschi, Giovanni. *Comrade Don Camillo*. Farrar, Straus, 1964.
*⎯⎯⎯⎯. *Don Camillo and His Flock*. Pellegrini & Cudahy, 1952.
*⎯⎯⎯⎯. *The Little World of Don Camillo*. Pelligrini & Cudahy, 1950.

Halevy, L. *Abbé Constantin*. Calmann-Levy, (French) 1948.
*Hallack, Cecily. *The Happiness of Father Happe*. Kenedy, 1938.
Harland, H. *The Cardinal's Snuff-Box*. Dodd, Mead, 1934.
*Horgan, P. *Devil in the Desert*. Longmans, 1952.
Hudson, J. W. *Abbe Pierre*. Appleton, 1922.

*Janney, R. *The Miracle of the Bells*. Prentice-Hall, 1946.

*Kaye-Smith, S. *Superstition Corner*. Regnery, 1955.
Keneally, T. *Three Cheers for the Paraclete*. Viking, 1968.

Leckie, R. *Ordained*. Doubleday, 1969.
Lewis, M. *The Monk*. Grove Press, 1952.
Lindop, A. *The Singer Not the Song*. Appleton-Century-Crofts, 1953.

Manzoni, A. *The Betrothed*. Dutton, 1952.
McLaverty, M. *In This Thy Day*. Macmillan. 1947.
*Mannin, E. *Late Have I Loved Thee*. Putnam, 1948.
Marshall, B. *The Bishop*. Doubleday, 1969.
_____. *The Fair Bride*. Houghton Mifflin, 1953.
*_____. *Father Malachy's Miracle*. Doubleday, 1932.
*_____. *To Every Man a Penny*. Houghton Mifflin, 1949.
*_____. *The World, the Flesh and Father Smith*. Houghton Mifflin, 1945.
Mauriac, F. *The Lamb*. Farrar, Straus, 1955.
Mydans, S. *Thomas*. Doubleday, 1965.

*Novak, M. *The Tiber was Silver*. Doubleday, 1961.

O'Connor, E. *The Edge of Sadness*. Little, Brown, 1961.

*Pezeril, D. *Rue Notre Dame*. Sheed & Ward, 1953.
*Power, C. *The Encounter*. Wm. Sloane, 1950.
*Powers, J. F. *Morte d'Urban*. Doubleday, 1962.
*_____. *The Presence of Grace*. Doubleday, 1956.
*_____. *Prince of Darkness*. Doubleday, 1947.
Prescott, H. F. M. *Man on a Donkey: A chronicle*. Macmillan, 1952.

*Queffelec, H. *Island Priest*. Dutton, 1952.

Read, P. *Monk Dawson*. Lippincott, 1970.
*Robinson, H. M. *The Cardinal*. Simon & Schuster, 1950.
*Romaniello, J. *Bird of Sorrow*. Kenedy, 1956.
Roy, G. C. *Where Nests the Water Hen*. Harcourt, Brace, 1951.

*Schofield, W. *The Deer Cry: A Novel of Patrick of Eirinn.* Longmans, Green, 1948.
Sheehan, Patrick. *Luke Delmage.* Regnery. 1955.
———. *My New Curate,* Longmans, Green, 1942.
*Sheehy, M. S. *Priestly Heart.* Farrar, Straus. 1956.

Waddell, H. *Peter Abelard: A Novel.* Literary Guild, 1933.
Werfel, Franz. *Embezzled Heaven.* Viking, 1940.
West, M. *The Devil's Advocate.* Wm. Morris, 1959.
———. *The Shoes of the Fisherman: A Novel.* Morrow, 1963.
White, Helen C. *Not Built by Hands.* Macmillan, 1946.
———. *To the End of the World.* Macmillan, 1939.
Wise, E. V. *Long Tomorrow.* Appleton-Century. 1938.

*Ziegler, I. *The Nine Days of Father Serra.* Longmans, Green, 1951.

2 Priest-Saints: Biographies

"But then there comes the second series, also very varied, the series of priests that have really existed: the Saints, such as St. Vincent de Paul, Don Bosco, the Cure d'Ars and let us add Maximilian Kolbe (whom we will declare Blessed on Sunday) . . ."

*Dorcy, Mary Jean, Sr. *Master Albert: The Story of Albert the Great*. Sheed & Ward, 1955.

*Martindale, Cyril C. *The Vocation of Aloysius Gonzaga*. Sheed & Ward, 1945.

*Magaret, Helene. *A Kingdom and a Cross: St. Alphonsus Liguori*. Bruce, 1958.

*Beahn, John E. *A Rich Young Man. Saint Anthony of Padua*. Bruce, 1953.

Clausen, Sophronius. *St. Anthony: Doctor of the Gospel*. Franciscan Herald Press, 1961.

Habig, Marion A. *Everyman's Saint: Life, Cult, and Virtues of St. Anthony of Padua*. St. Anthony Guild Press, 1954.

*O'Brien, Isidore. *Enter St. Anthony: Life of the Wonder-Worker of Padua*. St. Anthony Guild Press, 1946.

*Augustine, St. *The Confessions of St. Augustine*. Modern Library, 1949 (Sheed & Ward, 1942).

Bourke, Vernon J. *Augustine's Quest for Wisdom: Life and Philosophy of the Bishop of Hippo*. Bruce, 1945.

*Lomask, Milton. *Saint Augustine and His Search for Faith*. Farrar, Straus, and Cudahy, 1957.

Van der Meer, Frederick. *Augustine the Bishop: The Life and Work of a Father of the Church*. Sheed & Ward, 1962.

O'Meara, John J. *The Young Augustine: The Growth of St. Augustine's Mind Up to His Conversion*. Longmans, Green, 1954.

Brodrick, James. *Robert Bellarmine: Saint and Scholar*. Newman, 1961.

Bernard of Clairvaux, *St. Bernard of Clairvaux: Seen Through His Selected Letters*. Regnery. 1953.

*Raymond, M., O.C.S.O. *The Family That Overtook Christ: The Saga of Citeaux*. Kenedy, 1942.

Wilham of St. Thierry, et al. *St. Bernard of Clairvaux*. Tr. by Geoffrey Webb & Adrian Walker. Newman, 1960.

Yeo, Margaret. *The Greatest of the Borgias*: About St. Francis Borgia, 1510–1572. Bruce, 1952.

Priest-Saints: Biographies

*Boyton, Neil. *The Blessed Friend of Youth: St. John Bosco.* Rev. ed. Macmillan, 1935.

*Doherty, Edward J. *Lambs in Wolfskins: The Conquering March of Don John Bosco.* Scribner, 1953.

*Kuhn, Anna. *The Quest of Don Bosco.* Bruce, 1942.

Sheppard, Lancelot C. *Don Bosco.* Newman, 1957.

Hallett, Paul H. *Catholic Reformer: A Life of St. Cajetan of Thiene.* Newman Press, 1959.

Martindale, Cyril C. *Life of St. Camillus.* Sheed & Ward, 1946.

*Gardiner, Harold C. *Edmund Campion: Hero of God's Underground.* Farrar, Straus & Cudahy, 1957.

*Waugh, Evelyn. *Edmund Campion.* Little, Brown, 1946.

Cloupeau, J. *In the Land of Taboos: Life of St. Peter Chanel, S. M.* St. Anthony Guild Press, 1957.

*Royer. F. *Saint Anthony Claret: Modern Prophet, and Healer.* Farrar, Straus & Cudahy, 1957.

Sargent, D. *The Assignment of Antonio Claret.* McMullen, 1948.

*Roos, Ann. *Peter Claver: Saint Among Slaves.* Farrar, Straus & Giroux, 1965.

Valtierra, Angel. *Peter Claver: Saint of the Slaves.* Newman, 1960.

MacManus, F. *Saint Columban.* Sheed & Ward, 1962.

Gheon, Henri. *St. Vincent Ferrer.* Sheed & Ward, 1954.

Machlem, M. *God Have Mercy: The Life of John Fisher of Rochester.* Oberon Press, 1967.

Reynolds, Ernest E. *Saint John Fisher.* Kenedy, 1955.

*Bregy, K. *The Story of St. Francis de Sales: Patron of Catholic Writers.* Bruce, 1958.

Muller, Michael. *St. Francis de Sales.* Sheed & Ward, 1938.

Woodgate, Mildred V. *Saint Francis de Sales.* Newman, 1961.

*McGratty, A. *The Fire of Francis Xavier. The Story of an Apostle.* Bruce, 1952.

*Purcell, M. *Don Francisco. The Story of St. Francis Xavier.* Newman, 1954.

*Royer, F. *St. Francis Solanus: Apostle to America.* St. Anthony Guild, 1955.

*Gumbley, W. *Parish Priests Among the Saints.* Newman, 1947.

Hollis, C. *St. Ignatius.* Sheed & Ward, 1945.

*Purcell, M. *The First Jesuit: St. Ignatius Loyola.* Newman, 1957.

*Lomask, M. *St. Isaac and the Indians.* Farrar, Straus & Cudahy, 1956.

*Talbot, F. *Saint Among Savages. The Life of Isaac Jogues.* Harper, 1935.

Steinmann, Jean. *St. Jerome and His Times.* Fides, 1959.

Hefer, John. *St. John Capistran: Reformer.* Herder, 1943.

Sargent, D. *Their Hearts Be Praised: The Life of St. John Eudes,* Kenedy, 1949.

Cristiani, L. *St. John of the Cross.* Doubleday, 1962.

Boresky, T. *Life of St. Josaphat: Martyr of the Union.* Comet, 1955.

*Winowska, M. *Our Lady's Fool: Father Maximilian Kolbe.* Newman, 1952.

———. (*The Death Camp Proved Him Real.* PROW. Kenosha, Wis., 1971. Title of revised edition.)

Carmignano, A. *St. Lawrence of Brindisi.* Newman, 1963.

*Homan, H. W. *The Star of Jacob.* The Story of the Venerable Francis Libermann. McKay, 1953.

Van Kaam, Adrian. *A Light to the Gentiles: The Life Story of the Venerable Francis Libermann.* Bruce, 1959.

Luddy, Ailbe, J. O. *Life of St. Malachy.* Dublin, Gill, 1950.

*Windeatt, M. *Our Lady's Slave. The Story of St. Louis Mary Grignon de Montfort.* Grail, 1950.

Gheon, H. *St. Martin of Tours.* Sheed & Ward, 1946.

*Curley, M. *Venerable John Neumann, C.SS.R.: Fourth Bishop of Philadelphia.* Crusader, 1952.

Burton, K. *In Heaven We Shall Rest. The Life of Vincenzo Pallotti.* Benziger, 1955.

MacNeill, Eoin *St. Patrick; Apostle of Ireland.* Sheed & Ward, 1934.

*Reynolds, Q. *The Life of St. Patrick.* Random House, 1955.

Giordani, I. *St. Paul: Apostle and Martyr.* Macmillan, 1946.

*Mary Elanore, M. *The Last Apostle.* Bruce, 1956.

Daniel-Rops, H. *Saint Paul, Apostle.* Fides, 1953.

Priest-Saints: Biographies

Ricciotti, G. *Paul the Apostle*. Bruce, 1952.
*Walsh, W. T. *Saint Peter, The Apostle*. Macmillan, 1948.
Brodrick, J. *Saint Peter Canisius, S.J.* Newman, 1950.
Lewis, D. B. W. *A Florentine Portrait: Saint Philip Benizi (1233–1285)*. Sheed & Ward, 1959.
Joahandeau, M. *St. Philip Neri*. Harper, 1960.
*Maynard, T. *Mystic in Motley: The Life of St. Philip Neri*. Bruce, 1946.
*Burton, K. *The Great Mantle: The Life of Giuseppi M. Sarto, Pope Pius X*. Longmans, Green, 1950.
*Dal-Gal, H. *Pius X: The Life Story of the Beatus*. Newman, 1954.
*Hunermann, W. *Flame of White: A Life of St. Pius X*. Franciscan Herald, 1959.
*Giordani, I. *Pius X: A Country Priest*. Bruce, 1954.
Curtayne, A. *The Trial of Oliver Plunkett*. Sheed & Ward, 1953.
Grieco, R. *The Listening Heart: Life of John B. Scalabrini*. Society of St. Charles, 1965.
*Devlin, C. *The Life of Robert Southwell: Poet and Martyr*. Farrar, Straus, 1956.
*Moseley, D. H. *Blessed Robert Southwell*. Sheed & Ward, 1957.
Fischer, M. *Grey Dawns and Red*. About Bl. Theophane Venard. Sheed & Ward, 1939.
*Carroll, M. *Time Cannot Dim*. About Thomas Aquinas. Regnery, 1955.
Chesterton, G. K. *St. Thomas Aquinas*. Sheed & Ward, 1933.
*Grabman, M. *The Interior Life of St. Thomas Aquinas*. Bruce, 1951.
Maritain, J. *The Angelic Doctor: The Life and Thought of St. Thomas Aquinas*. Longmans, Green, 1931.
*Maritain, R. *The Angel of the Schools, St. Thomas Aquinas*. Sheed & Ward, 1955.
*Duggan, A. *My Life for My Sheep*. About St. Thomas à Becket. Coward-McAnn, 1955.
*Betz, Eva. *The Man Who Fought the Devil*. St. Anthony Guild, 1958.
Fourrey, R. *The Curè d'Ars*. Kenedy, 1959.

Gheon, H. *The Secret of the Curè d'Ars.* Longmans, Green, 1929.
*Pezeril, D. *Blessed and Poor: The Spiritual Odyssey of the Curè d'Ars.* Pantheon, 1961.
Trochu, F. *The Curè d'Ars.* Newman, 1950.
*Trouncer, M. *Saint Jean-Marie Vianney, Curè d'Ars.* Sheed & Ward, 1959.
*Windeatt, M. *The Parish Priest of Ars.* Grail, 1947.
*Daniel-Rops, H. *Monsieur Vincent: The Story of St. Vincent de Paul.* Hawthorn, 1961.
Maynard, T. *Apostle of Charity: The Life of St. Vincent de Paul.* Dial, 1939.
*Purcell, M. *The World of Monsieur Vincent.* Scribners, 1963.

3 Priests: Biographies

"... And alongside these great figures (and there are thousands of them) there are other dear and modest images of good, holy priests, that each of us, we suppose, has met along his own path: parish priests, religious, teachers, assistants, chaplains ... They have added to the specifically ministerial charismatic gift of the Word of God and of sacramental Grace, something of their own, their own humble, human way of inviting, welcoming, listening, admonishing, sympathizing, consoling, understanding, doing good ..."

Dominian, Helen. *Apostle of Brazil: The Biography of Padre Jose de Anchieta, S.J. (1534–1597).* Exposition, 1958.

Schauinger, J. Herman. *Stephen T. Badin: Priest in the Wilderness.* Bruce, 1956.

*Jamison, James K. *By Cross and Anchor: The Story of Frederic Baraga on Lake Superior.* St. Anthony Guild Press, 1946.

*Betz, E. *Virgil Barber, New England Pied Piper.* Kenedy, 1963.

*Carey, Kenan. *The Apostle of the Second Spring.* Paulist Press, 1945.

*Gwynn, Denis R. *Father Dominic Barberi: Desmond.* Stapleton, 1948.

Barrett, E. B. *A Shepherd Without Sheep.* Bruce, 1956.

*_____. *Shepherds in the Mist.* McMullen, 1949.

*Newcomb, Covello. *The Broken Sword. The Story of Fray Bartolome de Las Casas.* Dodd, Mead, 1955.

Peters, W. *The Life of Benedict XV.* Bruce, 1959.

Rope, Henry E. G. *Benedict XV, Pope of Peace.* London, John Gifford, 1941.

Benson, Arthur C. *Hugh, Memories of a Brother.* Longmans, Green, 1916.

Holy Cross Quarterly. *On the Berrigan Brothers.* Holy Cross College, 1971.

Santen, Herman. *Father Bishop: Founder of the Glenmary Home Missioners.* Bruce, 1960.

*Borelli, Mario. *A Street Lamp and the Stars. The Autobiography of Don Borelli of Naples.* Coward-McCann, 1963.

Reynolds, E. E. *Bossuet.* Doubleday. 1963.

Brodrick, Alan H. *Father of Prehistory: The Abbè Henri Breuil: His Life and Times.* Morrow, 1963.

Carrouges, Michel. *Pere Jacques.* About Bunel, Lucien, 1900–1945, Carmelite, WW II prisoner. Macmillan, 1961.

Lane, Raymond A. *Ambassador in Chains. The Life of Bishop Patrick James Byrne (1888–1950), Apostolic Delegate to the Republic of Korea.* Kenedy, 1955.

Priests: Biographies 33

Broucher, J. *Dom Helder Camara: The Violence of a Peacemaker.* Orbis, 1970.
*DeLaBedoyere, M. *The Cardijn Story.* Bruce, 1959.
Melville, A. *John Carroll of Baltimore.* Scribners. 1955.
Trappes-Lomax, Michael. *Bishop Challoner: A Biographical Study.* Longmans, Green, 1947.
Burton, Katherine. *Chaminade, Apostle of Mary: Founder of the Society of Mary,* Bruce, 1949.
Melville, Annabelle. *Jean Lefebvre de Cheverus, 1768–1836.* Bruce, 1958.
Ledit, Joseph *Archbishop John Baptist Cieplak.* Montreal, Palm Publishers, 1963.
*Ciszek, W. *With God in Russia.* McGraw-Hill, 1964.
Collins, William. *Out of the Depths: The Story of a Priest-Patient in a Mental Hospital.* Doubleday, 1971.
*Armitage, Angus. *Sun, Stand Thou Still. The Life and Work of Copernicus, the Astronomer.* H. Schuman, Life of Science Library, 1947.
Raymond, A. *Waterfront Priest.* Holt, 1955.
Tull, C. *Father Coughlin and the New Deal.* Syracuse University Press, 1965.
*Crosbie, R. *March Till They Die.* Dublin: Browne & Nolan, 1955.
Cutler, J. *Cardinal Cushing of Boston.* Hawthorn, 1970.
*Dever, J. *Cushing of Boston.* Bruce Humphries, 1965.
*Farrow, J. *Damien the Leper.* Sheed & Ward, 1937.
Jacks, Leo V. *Claude Dubuis, Bishop of Galveston.* Herder, 1946.
*Bishop, J. *Fighting Father Duffy.* Farrar, Straus & Giroux, 1956.
*Dupeyrat, Andre. *Savage Papua, A Missionary Among Cannibals.* Dutton, 1954.
*Grant, Dorothy F. *John England, American Christopher.* Bruce, 1949.
*Betz, E. *Priest on Horseback, Father Farmer 1720–1786.* Sheed & Ward, 1958.
*Father X (Hilkert, R.) *Everybody Calls Me Father.* Sheed & Ward, 1951.

Schauinger, J. *Cathedrals in the Wilderness.* About Benedict J. Flaget. Bruce, 1952.
*Oursler, F. *Father Flanagan of Boys Town.* Doubleday, 1949.
*Foley, A. *God's Men of Color: The Colored Catholic Priests.* Farrar, Straus, 1955.
*Cole, M. *Summer in the City.* Kenedy, 1968.
Gallagher, J. P. *Scarlet Pimpernel of the Vatican.* Coward-McCann, 1967.
*Sargent, D. *Mitri, or the Story of Prince Demetrius A. Gallitzin.* Longmans, Green, 1945.
Leslie, Shane. *Cardinal Gasquet, A Memoir.* Kenedy, 1953.
*Gerard, J. *The Autobiography of a Hunted Priest.* Pellegrini & Cudahy, 1952.
*Palmer, G. *God's Underground.* Appleton-Century-Crofts, 1949.
Ellis, John Tracy. *The Life of James Cardinal Gibbons, Archbishop of Baltimore, 1834–1921.* 2 vols. Bruce, 1952.
*Newcomb, C. *Larger Than the Sky: A Story of James Cardinal Gibbons.* Longmans, Green, 1943.
*Tehan, A. *Prince of Democracy, James Cardinal Gibbons.* Hanover House, 1962.
Girandola, A. *The Most Defiant Priest.* Crown, 1968.
*Goldman, G. *The Shadow of His Wings.* Franciscan Herald Press, 1964.
*Greene, R. *Calvary in China.* Putnam, 1953.
Hayne, D. *Batter My Heart.* Alfred A. Knopf, 1963.
*Foley, A. *Bishop Healy, Beloved Outcaste.* Farrar, Straus & Young, 1954.
Burton, K. *Celestial Homespun: The Life of Isaac Thomas Hecker.* Longmans, Green, 1943.
Holden, Vincent F. *The Yankee Paul, Isaac Thomas Hecker.* Bruce, 1958.
*Bonn, J. *Gates of Dannemora.* About Ambrose R. Hyland, Doubleday, 1951.
Moynihan, J. *The Life of Archbishop John Ireland.* Harper, 1953.
*Aradi, Zsolt. *Pope John XXIII: An Authoritative Biography.* Farrar, Straus, 1959.

Priests: Biographies

*Murphy, F. X. *Pope John XXIII Comes to the Vatican.* McBride, 1959.
John XXIII, Pope. *Journal of a Soul.* McGraw-Hill, 1965.
Trevor, Meriol *Pope John.* Doubleday, 1967.
*Kane, G. *Why I Became a Priest.* Newman, 1952.
*Tonne, A. *The Story of Chaplain Kapaun.* Didde, 1954.
Ahern, Patrick H. *The Life of John J. Keane, Educator and Archbishop, 1838–1915.* Bruce, 1955.
Keller, James *To Light a Candle: The Autobiography of James Keller, Founder of the Christophers.* Doubleday, 1963.
Kelley, Francis C. *The Bishop Jots It Down: An Autobiographical Strain on Memories.* Harper, 1939.
Corbishley, T. *Ronald Knox, the Priest.* Sheed & Ward, 1965.
Knox, R. *A Spiritual Aeneid.* Newman, 1948.
*Winowska, M. *Our Lady's Fool: Father Maximilian Kolbe.* Newman, 1952.
(*The Death Camp Proved Him Real.* PROW, Kenosha, Wis. 1971. Title of revised edition.)
Sheppard, L. *Lacordaire.* Macmillan, 1964.
LaFarge, J. *An American Amen, a Statement of Hope.* Farrar, Straus, 1958.
———. *The Manner Is Ordinary.* Harcourt, Brace, 1954.
Lauro, J. *Action Priest.* Wm. Morrow, 1971.
Pies, O. *The Victory of Father Karl.* Farrar, Straus & Cudahy, 1957.
Burton, K. *Leo the Thirteenth: The First Modern Pope.* McKay, 1962.
*Kiefer, W. *Leo XIII, a Light from Heaven.* Bruce, 1961.
Lepp, I. *From Karl Marx to Jesus Christ.* Sheed & Ward, 1958.
*Huber, G. *My Door Is Always Open.* About Cardinal Lercaro. Fides, 1959.
*Leow, J. *Mission to the Poorest.* Sheed & Ward, 1950.
*Lord, D. *Letters to My Lord.* Herder & Herder, 1969.
———. *Played by Ear.* Loyola University Press, 1956.
*McGoey, J. *Nor Scrip Nor Shoes.* Little, Brown, 1958.
Walsh, J. E. *The Man on Joss Stick Alley.* Longmans, Green, 1947.

*Maguire, W. *The Captain Wears a Cross.* Macmillan, 1943.
*_____. *Rig for Church.* Macmillan, 1942.
Leslie, Shane *Henry Edward Manning: His Life and Labours.* Kenedy, 1921.
Repplier, A. *Pere Marquette.* Doubleday, 1929.
Martin Descalzo, J. *A Priest Confesses.* Academy Guild Press, 1960.
Bocquet, M. *The Firebrand: The Life of Father Mateo Crawley-Boevey, SS.CC.* Corda, 1966.
Rogers, P. *Father Theobald Mathew, Apostle of Temperance.* Longmans, 1945.
Meadows, D. *Obedient Men.* Appleton-Century-Crofts, 1954.
Mercier, D. J. *Cardinal Mercier's Own Story.* Doran, 1920.
*Buehrle, M. *Raphael Cardinal Merry Del Val.* Bruce, 1957.
*Merton, T. *The Seven-Story Mountain.* Harcourt, Brace, 1948.
*Michonneau, G. *Revolution in a City Parish.* Newman, 1950.
*Fabian, B. *Cardinal Mindszenty: The Story of a Modern Martyr.* Scribner, 1949.
*Mojica, J. F. *I, a Sinner.* Franciscan Herald Press, 1963.
Moore, E. *Roman Collar.* Macmillan, 1950.
MacEoin, G. *Father Moreau, Founder of Holy Cross.* Bruce, 1962.
Caraman, P. *Henry Morse.* Farrar, Straus, 1957.
Barry, C. J. *American Nuncio: Cardinal Aloisius Muench.* St. John's University, 1969.
*Mulvey, T. *These Are Your Sons.* McGraw-Hill, 1952.
Murphy, E. *Yankee Priest: An Autobiographical Journey.* Doubleday, 1952.
*Myers, R. *The Greatest Calling: A Presentation of the Priesthood.* McMullen, 1951.
Magaret, H. *Giant in the Wilderness: A Biography of Father Charles Nerinckx.* Bruce, 1952.
*Newcomb, C. *The Red Hat: A Story of John Henry Newman.* Longmans, 1945.
O'Faolain, S. *Newman's Way: The Odyssey of John H. Newman.* Devin-Adair, 1952.
Ward, Maisie. *Young Mr. Newman.* Sheed & Ward, 1948.

Priests: Biographies

Ginder, R. *With Ink and Crozier: A Biography of John F. Noll.* Our Sunday Visitor, 1952.

Wayman, D. *Cardinal O'Connell of Boston.* Farrar, Straus & Young, 1955.

Shaw, J. G. *Edwin Vincent O'Hara, American Prelate.* Farrar, Straus, 1957.

*Palmer, G. *God's Underground in Asia.* Appleton-Century-Crofts, 1953.

*Clancy, J. *Apostle for Our Times: Pope Paul VI.* Kenedy, 1963.

Gannon, D. *Father Paul of Graymoor.* Macmillan, 1951.

*Perrin, Henri. *Priest-Workman in Germany.* Sheed & Ward, 1948.

Pfau, R. *Prodigal Shepherd.* Lippincott, 1958.

*Pierre, Abbe. *Abbe Pierre Speaks.* Sheed & Ward, 1956.

Furlan, W. *In Charity Unfeigned: The Life of Father Francis X. Pierz.* Diocese of St. Cloud, 1952.

*Vehenne, H. *The Story of Father Dominic Pire. Winner of the Nobel Peace Prize,* 1961.

*Parente, Pascal P. *A City on a Mountain, Padre Pio of Pietrelcina, O.F.M. Cap.* Grail, 1952.

Pittini, R. *Memories in My Blindness.* Salesiana, 1952.

*Thornton, F. *Cross Upon Cross: The Life of Pope Pius IX.* Benziger, 1955.

*Aradi, Zsolt. *Pius XI, The Pope and the Man.* Hanover House, 1958.

Halecki, O. *Eugenio Pacelli, Pope of Peace.* Creative Age Press, 1951.

*Hatch, A. *Crown of Glory: The Life of Pope Pius XII.* Hawthorn, 1958.

Tardini, D. Card. *Memories of Pius XII.* Newman, 1961.

*Murrett, J. *Tar Heel Apostle, Thomas F. Price, Co-Founder of Maryknoll.* Longmans, Green, 1944.

*Blount, M. *God's Jester: The Story of the Life and Martyrdom of Father Michael Pro, S.J.* Benziger, 1930.

*Forrest, M. *The Life of Father Pro.* Radio Replies Press, 1945.

*Royer, F. *Padre Pro.* Kenedy, 1954.

Reinhold, H. A. *H.A.R.* Herder & Herder, 1968.

Cronin, V. *The Wise Man from the West*, About Fr. Ricci, S.J. Dutton, 1955.

Mast, Dolorita, Sr. *Always the Priest: The Life of Gabriel Richard*, S.S. Helicon, 1965.

Woodford, F. *Gabriel Richard: Frontier Ambassador*. Catholic Family Book Club, 1959.

O'Connell, D. P. *Richelieu*. World Publishers, 1968.

Peyton, P. *All for Her, the Autobiography of Father Patrick Peyton, C.S.C.* Doubleday, 1967.

*Rigney, H. *Four Years in a Red Hell*. Regnery, 1956.

*Raymond, M. *Three Religious Rebels, Forefathers of the Trappists*. Kenedy, 1944.

*Romaniello, J. *Bird of Sorrow*. Kenedy, 1956.

*Russell, S. *A Man in the Middle*. Pflaum, 1969.

Broderick, F. *Right Reverend New Dealer*. About Fr. J. A. Ryan. Macmillan, 1963.

Ryan, T. *Jesuits Under Fire in the Siege of Hong Kong*. Burns, Oates & Washbourne, 1941.

*Sampson, F. *Look Out Below!* Catholic University Press, 1948.

*———. *Paratrooper Padre*. Catholic University Press, 1948.

*Bolton, Ivy. *Father Junipero Serra*. Messner, 1954.

Englebert, O. *The Last of the Conquistadors, Junipero Serra*. Harcourt, Brace, 1956.

*Martini, Teri. *Sandals on the Golden Highway: A Life of Junipero Serra*. St. Anthony Guild Press, 1959.

Sheeran, J. *Confederate Chaplain: A War Journal*. Bruce, 1960.

*Treat, R. *Bishop Sheil and the CYO*. Messner, 1951.

Durkin, J. *General Sherman's Son*. Farrar, Straus & Cudahy. 1959.

Ward, J. *Thomas Edward Shields*. Scribner, 1947.

Maynard, T. *The Reed and the Rock: Portrait of Simon Brute*. Longmans, 1942.

Simon, M. R. *The Glory of Thy People: The Story of a Conversion*. Macmillan, 1948

Smyth, B. *But Not Conquered*. Newman Press, 1958.

*Cross, C. *Soldiers of God*. Dutton, 1945.

Priests: Biographies

Ellis, J. T. *John Lancaster Spaulding: First Bishop of Peoria.* Bruce, 1961.

*Gannon, R. *The Cardinal Spellman Story.* Doubleday, 1962.

Pattee, R. *The Case of Cardinal Aloysius Stepinac.* Bruce, 1953.

*Burton, K. *No Shadow of Turning: The Life of James Kent Stone* (Father Fidelis). Longmans, Green, 1949.

*Buehrle, M. *The Cardinal Stritch Story.* Bruce, 1959.

*Suigo, C. *In the Land of Mao Tse-Tung.* Allen & Unwin, 1953.

*Lattin, H. *The Peasant Boy Who Became Pope: Story of Gerbert.* Schuman, 1951.

DeTerra, H. *Memories of Teilhard de Chardin.* Harper, 1965.

Raven, C. *Teilhard de Chardin, Scientist and Seer.* Harper, 1962.

*Tennien, M. *No Secret is Safe.* Farrar, Straus & Young, 1952.

Boyle, G. *Father Tompkins of Nova Scotia.* Kenedy, 1953.

Van Zeller, H. *One Foot in the Cradle: An Autobiography.* Holt, Rinehart, 1965.

Richardson, M. *Joseph Varin, Soldier.* Catholic Book Club, 1953.

Gannon, M. *Rebel Bishop. The Life of Augustin Verot.* Bruce, 1964.

Sargent, D. *All the Day Long.* About J. A. Walsh. Longmans Green, 1941.

*Kerrison, R. *Bishop Walsh of Maryknoll.* About J. E. Walsh. Putnam, 1962.

Walsh, J. J. *Those Splendid Priests.* Sears & Co., 1926.

*Grant, D. *War is My Parish: Anecdote and Comment.* Bruce, 1944.

Murray, J. C. *One of a Kind: Essays in Tribute to Gustave Weigel.* Dimension, 1967.

Weston, W. *An Autobiography for the Jesuit Underground.* Farrar, Straus & Cudahy, 1955.

Gwynn, Denis. *Cardinal Wiseman.* Burns Oates & Washbourne, 1929.

Ferguson, Charles. *Naked to Mine Enemies: The Life of Cardinal Wolsey.* Little, Brown, 1958.

Weber, R. *Notre Dame's John Zahm.* University of Notre Dame Press, 1961.

4 The Priesthood

WRITINGS PRIOR TO VATICAN COUNCIL II

"The priest is the Ambassador of Christ. 'For Christ, therefore, we are ambassadors, God as it were exhorting by us.' (1 Cor. 3:9) As there is scarcely any public office more honorable or more expressive of a sovereign's esteem and confidence than that of ambassador, so there is hardly any title in the hierarchy which conveys with it more dignity and responsibility than that of Christ's legate. The envoy of Jesus Christ upholds and vindicates the rights and prerogatives of God among the people to whom he is sent, just as a minister plenipotentiary of the civil government sustains the power and majesty of the nation that he represents. He is furnished with the credentials of a divine embassy, and is enpowered to prescribe the conditions on which men may enter into a treaty of reconciliation and peace with the King of Kings." (Gibbons, James Cardinal. The Ambassador of Christ. *New York: John Murphy & Company, 1896, p. 15)*

Alphonsus de Liguori, St. *Dignity and Duties of the Priest;* or *Selva. A Collection of Materials for Ecclesiastical Retreats.* Benziger, 1889.

Bacuez, L. *Major Orders.* B. Herder, 1913.
Biskupek, A. *Priesthood. Conferences on the Rite of Ordination.* Herder, 1946.
Boylan, M. E. *The Priest's Way to God.* Newman, 1963.
———— *The Spiritual Life of the Priest.* Paulist-Newman, 1962.
Bruneau, J. *Our Priesthood.* Murphy, 1929.

Centre de Pastorale Liturgique. *The Sacrament of Holy Orders.* Liturgical Press, 1962.
Charue, A. M. *The Diocesan Clergy: History and Spirituality.* Desclee, 1963.
Cicognani, A. *The Priest in the Epistles of St. Paul.* St. Anthony Guild Press, 1944.
Cohausz, O. *The Priest and St. Paul.* Benziger, 1927.
Connell, F. J. *Spiritual and Pastoral Conferences to Priests.* Newman, 1962.
Courtois, G. *The Young Priest.* Herder & Herder, 1965.
Crawley-Boevey, Mateo. *Father Mateo Speaks to Priests on Priestly Perfection.* Newman, 1961.
*Cushing, R. *That They May Know Thee.* Newman, 1956.

Dillenschneider, C. *Christ the One Priest and We His Priests.* Herder, 1964.
Donahue, G. *The Secular Priesthood.* Stratford, 1932.
Dougherty, J. *Unto the Altar of God.* Exposition, 1966.

Eder, K. *On the Path of Holiness: Essays Portraying the Spirit and Activity of the Secular Priesthood.* B. Herder, 1932.
*Engleman, J. *The Catholic Priest.* Lothrop, Lee & Shephard, 1961.

The Priesthood 43

Fenton, J. *The Concept of the Diocesan Priesthood.* Bruce, 1951.

Garesche, E. *The Priest.* Bruce, 1930.
Garrigou-Lagrange, R. *The Priest in Union with Christ.* Newman, 1954.
*Gibbons, J. *The Ambassador of Christ.* Murphy, 1896.
*Goebel, B. *Seven Steps to the Altar.* Sheed & Ward, 1963.

Heston, E. L. *Priest of the Fathers.* Bruce, 1945.
Holland, C. *The Shepherd and His Flock.* McKay, 1953.

Janssen, J. *Priestly Zeal for Souls.* Pustet, 1946.
John Chrysostom, St. *On the Priesthood.* Newman, 1943.
*John Eudes, St. *The Priest: His Dignity and Obligations.* Kenedy, 1947.

*Kane, G. L. *Meeting the Vocation Crisis.* Newman, 1956.
*———. *Why I Became a Priest.* Newman, 1952.
Kassiepe, M. *Priestly Beatitudes.* Herder, 1953.
Keatinge, J. *The Priest: His Character and Work.* Benziger, 1903.
*Keller, J. *The Priest and a World Vision.* The Christophers, 1946.
Kelley, F. *Sacerdos and Pontifex. Letters to a Bishop-Elect.* St. Anthony Guild, 1940.
Kerby, W. J. *The Considerate Priest.* Catholic University Press, 1950.
———. *Prophets of the Better Hope.* Bruce, 1946.
Kirlin, J. L. *Priestly Virtue and Zeal.* Benziger, 1928.
*Klaver, R. *The Call to the Altar.* Our Sunday Visitor, 1960.
Knox, R. *Retreat for Priests.* Sheed & Ward, 1946.
———. *The Priestly Life.* Sheed & Ward, 1958.

*Lecuyer, J. *What is a Priest?* Hawthorn, 1959.
Leen, E. *The Voice of a Priest.* Sheed & Ward, 1946.
Liturgical Conference. "The Priesthood of Christ." *National Liturgical Week.* Loras College. August 20-23, 1951-1952.

Lovasik, L. *Priestly Holiness*. St. Paul, 1961.

Madden, W. J. *Discourses on Priesthood with Panegyric of St. Patrick*. Herder, 1903.
Mahoney, E. J. *Priest's Problems*. Benziger, 1958.
Manning, H. E. *The Eternal Priesthood*. Newman, (1883) & 1944.
Marcetteau, B. *The Priest's Companion*. Benziger, 1944.
Marmion, C. *Christ—The Ideal of the Priest*. Sands & Co., 1952.
*Masure, E. *Parish Priest*. Fides, 1955.
*McGoey, J. H. *Fathering Forth*. Bruce, 1958.
Middleton, J. *Christ and the Priest*. Benziger, 1928.
*Myers, R. *The Greatest Calling*. McMullen, 1951.

Nash, R. *The Priest at His Prieu-Dieu*. Newman, 1945.
Navagh, J. J. *The Apostolic Parish*. Kenedy, 1950.
Noppell, C. *Shepherd of Souls: The Pastoral Office in the Mystical Body of Christ*. B. Herder, 1959.

*O'Brien, J. *The Priesthood in a Changing World*. St. Anthony Guild, 1943.
O'Donnell, T. *The Priest of Today*. Benziger, 1910.

Pfliegler, M. *Priestly Existence*. Newman, 1957.
Phelan, M. *The Young Priest's Keepsake*. Benziger, 1909.
Plassman, Thomas. *The Priest's Way to God*. 2d ed. St. Anthony Guild, 1945.
*Poage, G. *Recruiting for Christ*. Bruce, 1952.
*_____. *Today's Vocation Crisis*. Newman, 1962.
Pohlschneider, J. *Adsum: A Bishop Speaks to His Priests*. Herder, 1962.

Retif, Louis & Andre. *The Church's Mission in the World*. Hawthorn, 1962.

Schaefer, W. *Keepers of the Eucharist*. Bruce, 1946.
Schrijvers, J. *With the Divine Retreat Master. A Message from Jesus to His Priest*. St. Anthony Guild, 1939.

Sellmair, J. *The Priest in the World.* Newman, 1954.
*Shaw, S. *Salt of the Earth.* Burns Oates & Washbourne, 1947.
*Spicq, C. *The Mystery of Godliness.* Fides, 1954.
Stockums, W. *Vocation to the Priesthood.* Herder, 1937.
*Suhard, E. *The Priest Among Men.* Fides, 1953.

*Trese, L. *A Man Approved.* Sheed & Ward, 1953.
*————. *Sanctified in Truth.* Sheed & Ward, 1961.
*————. *Tenders of the Flock.* Sheed & Ward, 1955.
*————. *Vessel of Clay.* Sheed & Ward, 1950.

*Urtasun, Joseph. *What Is a Bishop?* Hawthorn, 1962.

*Van Zeller, H. *The Gospel Priesthood.* Sheed & Ward, 1956.
Vaughan, J. *The Minister of Christ.* 2 vols. Wagner, 1926.

WRITINGS DURING AND AFTER VATICAN COUNCIL II (1962–1965)

"I say to you, then, that the mark of our times is the spirit of sacrifice. If you seek yourself, you will live in contradiction; if you seek to give yourself, you will live in harmony with the time, with its peculiar note. Priests are needed who know how to truly give themselves, truly multiply themselves, manifest the treasures that the Lord has poured into their hearts with culture, meditation, and above all with the graces of the sacrament of Holy Orders. We must be inexhaustible fountains. We must know how to speak in all tongues, reach everyone, answer all needs. This is a characteristic of our times.

To this characteristic is added another: our pastoral ministry in today's world acquires an eminently personal character.

Many years ago, canonical law more than the presence of the person made the ministry efficacious. The church bell and custom sufficed; the priest was considered almost a 'distant dignitary' by the faithful. Today this no longer holds true. To be of help you will have to join the people, know them, become their friends. The apostolate must become capillary, and whatever worth it has will be determined by the living and personal relationship extended to all those to whom you will preach the Kingdom and the grace of God. Without this personal giving of oneself, today's pastoral life will leave no imprint. This work, too, of course, requires great effort and great delicacy. It is not, though, an unbearable load. It implies above all that our great authority, our high dignity, becomes what the Lord wished it to be—service to others, humility, a friendship which becomes dialogue, heart speaking to heart, person to person. Learn this work and you will be truly pastors and teachers, guides of souls; and if you do not, you will be an empty 'bleating voice' heard by no one." (*Montini, Giovanni Battista Cardinal,* The Priest. *Helicon, 1965, pp. 34–35.*)

Abbott, W. M., ed. *The Documents of Vatican II.* Herder & Herder, 1966.
Anciaux, P. *The Episcopate in the Church.* Alba House, 1965.
Audet, J. *Structures of the Christian Priesthood.* Sheed & Ward, 1967.

Bastian, R. *Priesthood and Ministry.* Paulist Press, 1969.
*Blomjous, J. *Priesthood in Crisis.* Bruce, 1969.
*Bordelon, M. *The Parish in Time of Change.* Fides, 1967.
*Brown, R. A. *Priest and Bishop: Biblical Reflections.* Paulist Press, 1970.
Bunnik, R. *Priests for Tomorrow.* Holt, Rinehart and Winston, 1969.

Colaianni, J. *Married Priests and Married Nuns.* McGraw-Hill, 1968.
*Congar, Y. *A Gospel Priesthood.* Herder & Herder, 1967.
*Congregation for Catholic Education. *The Basic Plan for Priestly Formation.* (Ratio fundamentalis institutionis sacerdotalis). March 16, 1970. National Conference of Catholic Bishops.

*D'Arcy, P. *The Genius of the Apostolate.* Sheed & Ward, 1965.
Dillenschneider, C. *The Holy Spirit and the Priest.* Herder, 1965.

Ellis, J. T., ed. *The Catholic Priest in the United States: historical investigations.* St. John's University Press, 1971.

*Fichter, J. *America's Forgotten Priests.* Harper & Row, 1968.
* _____. *Priests and People.* Sheed & Ward, 1965.
*Fransen, P. *Intelligent Theology* (Vol. 2, "Confirmation and Priesthood"). Franciscan Herald, 1969.
*Greeley, A. *New Horizons for the Priesthood.* Sheed & Ward, 1970.
* _____. *Priests for Tomorrow.* Ave Maria Press, 1964.

* ———. *Uncertain Trumpet: The Priest in Modern America.* Sheed & Ward, 1968.
* ———. *Priests in the United States: Reflections on a Survey.* Doubleday, 1972.

Hebert, A. J. *Priestly Celibacy—Recurrent Battle and Lasting Values.* Lumen Christi Press, 1971.
Hermand, P. *The Priest: Celibate or Married.* Helicon, 1965.
Hildebrand, P. von. *Celibacy and the Crisis of Faith.* Franciscan Herald Press, 1971.

*Jungmann, J. *Announcing the Word of God.* Herder & Herder, 1967.

Karrer, O. *The Kingdom of God Today.* Herder & Herder, 1964.
*Kennedy, E. *Comfort My People.* Sheed & Ward, 1968.

*Lash, N. *His Presence in the World.* Pflaum, 1968.
*Leclercq, J. *Man of God for Others.* Newman, 1968.

*McGoey, J. *The Uncertain Sound.* Bruce, 1967.
*Mohler, J. *The Origin and Evolution of the Priesthood.* Alba House, 1970.

National Conference of Catholic Bishops. *The Catholic Priest in the United States—Psychological Investigations.* The Loyola University Study directed by Eugene C. Kennedy, M.M., Ph.D., and Victor J. Heckler, Ph.D. United States Catholic Conference (USCC), 1972.
———. *The Catholic Priest in the United States—Sociological Investigations.* The National Opinion Research Center Study, the University of Chicago, directed by Rev. Andrew M. Greeley. USCC, 1972.
* ———. *Study on Priestly Life and Ministry.* Summaries of the Ad Hoc Bishops' Subcommittees on History, Sociology, Psychology. USCC, 1971.
Nouwen, H. J. *Creative Ministry.* Doubleday, 1971.

O'Neill, D. *The Priest in Crisis: A Study of Role Change.* Pflaum, 1968.

———. *Priestly Celibacy and Maturity.* Sheed & Ward, 1965.

*Paul VI, Pope. *The Priest.* Helicon, 1965. (Listed under Montini, G.)

Pellegrino, M. *The True Priest: The Priesthood as Preached and Practiced by St. Augustine;* by A. Gibson. Philosophical Library, 1968.

Rahner, K. ed. *The Identity of the Priest.* Paulist Press, 1969.

Rahner, K. *Servants of the Lord.* Herder & Herder, 1968.

———. *Theology for Renewal: Bishops, Priests, Laity.* Sheed & Ward, 1964.

*Ratzinger, J. *Priestly Ministry: A Search for Its Meaning.* The Sentinel Press, 1971. (Reprinted from *Emmanuel*, vol. 76, nos. 11 and 12, 1970.)

*Retif, L. *The Church's Mission in the World Today.* Vol. 102. Hawthorne, 1962.

Rihn, R. *The Priestly Amen.* Sheed & Ward, 1965.

Romb, A. W. *As One Who Serves.* Bruce, 1966.

Schelke, K. *Discipleship and Priesthood.* Herder & Herder, 1965.

Schillebeeckx, E. *Celibacy.* Sheed & Ward, 1968.

Simonet, A. *The Priest and His Bishop.* Herder & Herder, 1969.

*Sloyan, G. *Secular Priest in the New Church.* Herder & Herder, 1967.

*Suenens, L. *Coresponsibility in the Church.* Herder & Herder, 1968.

*Tartre, R. *The Postconciliar Priest.* Kenedy, 1966.

Thils, G. *The Diocesan Priest: The Nature and Spirituality of the Diocesan Clergy.* Fides, 1964.

Vatican Council II, (1962–1965). *Constitutiones-Decreta-Declarationes.* Vaticanum, 2 vols. 1967.

5 The Priesthood in Papal Documents

MAJOR DOCUMENTS—TWENTIETH CENTURY

". . . . *Beloved sons, we speak to you in the first place that we may incite you to that sanctity of life which the dignity of your office demands. For, whoever becomes a priest, is a priest, not for himself alone but for others: 'for every high priest taken from among men is appointed for men in the things pertaining to God'* (Heb. 5:1). *This Christ indicated when, to show what should be the priest's conduct, He used to compare him to salt and to light. The priest, then is the salt of the earth and the light of the world. Surely all know that he becomes this by teaching the truths of Christ, but who does not likewise know that his instruction is almost for nothing, unless he proves by his works what he preaches. . . ."* (Haerent Animo, St. Pius X, August 4, 1908)

"The priest, according to the magnificent definition given by St. Paul, is indeed a man Ex hominibus Assumptus, 'taken from amongst men,' yet pro hominibus constituitur in his quae sunt ad Deum, 'ordained for men in the things that appertain to God': his office is not for human things, and things that pass away, however lofty and valuable these things, may seem; but for things divine and enduring. These eternal things may, perhaps, through ignorance, be scorned and condemned, or even attacked with diabolical fury and malice, as sad experience has often proved, and proves even today;

but they always continue to hold the first place in the aspirations, individual and social, of humanity, because the human heart feels irresistibly it is made for God and is restless till it rests in Him." (*Ad Catholici Sacerdotii* [*On the Catholic priesthood*], Pius XI, December 20, 1935)

Abbreviations of Magazines Cited

A.A.S.—Acta Apostolicae Sedis
A.E.R.—American Ecclesiastical Review
A.S.S.—Acta Sanctae Sedis
Ave—Ave Maria
C. Lawyer—Catholic Lawyer
Cath. Mind—Catholic Mind
Clergy R.—Clergy Review
Doc. Cath.—Documentation Catholique
Dominicana—Dominicana
Eccles. Rev.—Ecclesiastical Review
Emmanuel—Emmanuel
Furrow—Furrow
H.P.R.—Homiletic and Pastoral Review
Jurist—Jurist
Liguorian—Liguorian
Marianum—Marianum
OL Dig.—Our Lady's Digest
OR (Engl.)—L'Osservatore Romuno (English edition)
Priest—The Priest
R. Rel.—Review for Religious
St. Meinrad Essays—St. Meinrad Essays
Sisters—Sisters Today
Soc. Just.—Social Justice
Sursum Corda—Sursum Corda
TPS—The Pope Speaks
Unitas—Unitas
US Cath.—United States Catholic

1908, August 4. Pius X, 1903–1914. *Haerent Animo* (exhortation to the clergy).

Text: A.S.S. 41: no. 9, pp. 555–77.
    Cath. Mind 18, September 22, 1908.
    Eccl. Rev. 39: 396–416, October 1908.
also *Letter to Catholic Priests*. St. Anthony Guild, 1947.
    Bruneau, J. *Our Priesthood*. Murphy, 1929.
  in Yzermans, V., ed. *All Things in Christ*. Newman, 1954.
Commentary:
    Healy, Kilian, O. Carm. *Haerent Animo* (Pius X)—after fifty years.
    A.E.R. 139: 240-48, October 1958.
    Morris, B. Expectation of the Church; teaching of St. Pius X.
    Dominicana 43: 134–39, Summer 1958.

1935, December 20. Pius XI, 1922–1939. *Ad Catholici Sacerdotii* (encyclical, on the offices, powers, and obligations of the priesthood).

Text: A.A.S. 28: 5–53, January 1936.
    Eccl. Rev. 94: 262–95, March 1936.
    Cath. Mind 34: 41–79, February 8, 1936.
also O'Brien, J. *The Priesthood in a Changing World*. St. Anthony Guild, 1943.
  in *Sixteen Encyclicals of Pius XI*. NCWC. 1938.

1943, June 29. Pius XII, 1939–1958. *Mystici Corporis* (encyclical, on the Body of Christ).

Text: A.A.S. 35 (1943) 193–248, July 20, 1943.
    Cath Mind 41: 1–44, November 1943.

1947, November 30. Pius XII, 1939–1958. *Mediator Dei* (encyclical letter).

Text: A.A.S. 39: 521–600, December 2, 1947.
Cath. Mind 46: 321–88, June 1948.

1947, November 30. Pius XII, 1939–1958. *Sacramentum Ordinis* (apostolic exhortation).

Text: A.A.S. 40: 5–7, January 28, 1958.
Jurist 8: 362–65, July 1948.
H.P.R. 48: 691–93, June 1948.

1950, September 23. Pius XII, 1939–1958. *Menti Nostrae* (apostolic exhortation).

Text: A.A.S. 42: 658–704, October 2, 1950.
Cath. Mind 49: 37–64, January 1951.

1954, March 25. Pius XII, 1939-1958. *Sacra Virginitas* (encyclical letter).

Text: A.A.S. 46: 161–191, May 16, 1954.
A.E.R. 131: 41–67, July 1954. (Latin)
A.E.R. 130: 404–30, June 1954.
Cath. Mind 52: 491–512, August 1954.
TPS 1: 101–23, July 1954.

1954, May 31. Pius XII, 1939–1958. *Si Diligis* (address to some 350 Cardinals, Archbishops present in Rome for canonization of St. Pius X: on the teaching authority of bishops; lay theologians).

Text: A.A.S. 46: 313–17, June 30, 1954.
A.E.R. 131: 127–37, August, 1954.
TPS 1: 153–58, July, 1954.

1954, November 2. Pius XII, 1939–1958. *Magnificate Dominum* (address to some 250 Cardinals and Bishops in Rome: on the power of the bishops to rule and sanctify; sequel to *Si Diligis*).

Text: A.A.S. 46: 666–77, November 18, 1954.
A.E.R. 132: 52–63, January 1955.
Cath. Mind 53: 311–20, May 1955.
TPS 1: 375–85, Winter 1954.

1959, August 1. John XXIII, 1958–1963. *Sacerdotii Nostri Primordia* (encyclical letter, St. John Vianney, model for priestly spirituality and pastoral work).

Text: A.A.S. 51: 546–79, August 1959.
A.E.R. 141: 321–51, November 1959.
TPS 6: 7–33, Winter 1960.

1960, January 25. John XXIII, 1958–1963. The priest: sacred person-holy life (first address to Roman Synod).

Text: A.A.S. 52: 201–11, April, 1960.
TPS 6: 155–57, Spring, 1960.

1960, January 26. John XXIII, 1958–1963. The priestly character: head, heart and tongue (second address to Roman Synod).

Text: A.A.S. 52: 221–30, April 1960.
TPS 6: 157–59, Spring 1960.

1960, January 27. John XXIII, 1958–1963. On the pastoral mission of all the clergy (third address to Roman Synod).

Text: A.A.S. 52: 240–51, April 1960.
TPS 6: 159–61, Spring 1960.

1960, January 28. John XXIII, 1958–1963. Counsels for seminarians: walk worthily, nourishment from Scripture, the Psalms and prayer.

Text: *TPS* 6: 363–69, 1960.

1962, September 9. John XXIII, 1958–1963. To the spiritual directors of seminaries in Italy.

Text: A.A.S. 54: 673–78, October 1962.
TPS 8: 259–64, 1963.
R. Rel. 22: 257–62, May 1963.

1963, November 4. Paul VI, 1963–. *Il grande rito* (allocution at the celebration of the fourth centenary of the Council of Trent constitution on seminaries).

Text: A.A.S. 55: 1030–35, December 1963.
TPS 9: 234–38, 1964.

1963, November 4. Paul VI, 1963–. *Summi Dei Verbum* (apostolic letter on the four hundredth anniversary of establishment of seminaries by Council of Trent).

Text: A.A.S. 55: 979–95, December 1963.
TPS 9: 239–50, 1964.

1963, November 30. Paul VI. *Pastorale munus* (motu proprio, special faculties and privileges granted to local Ordinaries on a permanent basis).

Text: A.A.S. 56: 5–12, January 31, 1964.
Jurist 24: 99–106, January 1964.

1964, August 6. Paul VI. *Ecclesiam suam* (the Church, self-awareness; reform and dialogue).

Text: A.A.S. 56: 609–59, August 20, 1964.
Liguorian 52: 45–49, November 1964.
OL Dig. 20: 181–82, November-December 1964.

1965, September 3. Paul VI. *Mysterium Fidei* (encyclical letter, on the Eucharist, in the light of modern theology).

Text: A.A.S. 57: 753–74, October 30, 1965.
A.E.R. 153: 325–42, November 1965.
TPS 10: 309–28, Summer–Fall 1965.

1966, August 6. Paul VI. *Ecclesiae Sanctae* (motu proprio, for implementing the Council decrees on the pastoral office of bishops, the priestly ministry).

Text: A.A.S. 58: 757–87, October 24, 1966.
Cath. Mind 64: 50–64, November 1966.
   49–59, December 1966.
R. Rel. 25: 939–70, November 1966.
Jurist 27: 104–38, January 1967.
Sisters 38: 69–99, November 1966.
TPS 11: 376–400, 1966.

1967, June 24. Paul VI. *Sacerdotalis caelibatus* (encyclical letter, on the celibacy of the priest).

Text: A.A.S. 59: 657–97, August 7, 1967.
Cath. Mind 65: 46–65, October 1967.
Priest 23: 623–653, August 1967.
TPS 12: 291–319, 1967.

1970, February 2. Paul VI. Letter to Cardinal Jean Villot, Papal Secretary of State, concerning the Dutch Bishops' statement on priestly celibacy.

Text: A.A.S. 62: 98–103, February 20, 1970.
Cath. Mind 68: 2–6, April 1970.
OR (Engl.) no. 7 (98), 5, February 12, 1970.
TPS 15: 40–44, 1970.

1970, November 28. Paul VI. Address at the ordination of Asiatic priests at Luneta Park, Manila.

Text: A.A.S. 63: 28–30, January 30, 1971.

OR (Engl.) no. 50 (141) pp. 1–2, December 10, 1970.
Priest 27: 77–78, March 1971.

1970, December 8 Paul VI. Apostolic exhortation to all the bishops on the fifth anniversary of the close of the Second Vatican Council.

Text: A.A.S. 63: 97–106, February 27, 1971.
Cath. Mind 69: 48–55, March 1971.
OR (Engl.) no. 2 (145), pp. 1–3, January 14, 1971.
TPS 15: 324–32, 1971.

OTHER PAPAL DOCUMENTS

Pius XII (1939–1958)

"You will really become a leaven of salvation for the whole modern world to the extent that you are able to attain, under the guidance of Holy Mother the Church, the inexhaustible vigor of the eternal Word, Who became man to make men sharers in His divine nature. May every Pastor of souls approach the world in that same way, with intelligence, knowledge, and love, so that he may not be dragged down by the world to its own level, but may see his human words bringing it the liberating truth of God, the transcendent perfection of the Redeemer, Jesus.

May our Lord grant you an abundant increase of the 'spirit of Christ' and of the 'spirit of the Church' of Christ, that you may carry out this duty of yours fruitfully." (Di gran cuore, *Pius XII, September 14, 1956,* TPS 3: 391–92, April 1957)

1939, December 8. *Asperis commoti* (apostolic exhortation). To priests and clerics who have been called upon to serve in the armed forces of nations.

A.A.S. 31: 696–701, December 22, 1939.
Cath. Mind (Engl.) 38: 9–17, January 8, 1940.
H.P.R. (excerpts) 40: 671–72, March 1940.

1951, October 14. *De quelle consolation* (address). On the lay apostolate; the clergy and Catholic Action.
St. Meinrad Essays (Engl.) 11: 57–67, May 1956.

1953, October 14. *On this day* (address). Dedication of new North America College in Rome: on the priesthood.

English text: A.A.S. 45: 679–82, November 15, 1953.
 Cath. Mind 52: 62–64, January 1954.

1954, May 29. *Quest' ora di fulgente* (address). Canonization of Pius X. His accomplishments for the Church, the Eucharist, and canon law.

Text: A.A.S. 46: 307–13, June 30, 1954.
  A.E.R. 131: 120–26, August 1954.
  Cath. Mind 52: 551–56, September 1954.
  TPS 1: 147–52, July 1954.

1955, March 10. *Siano rese grazie* (address). To the pastors and Lenten preachers of Rome: on pastoral work; the spiritual life of parish priests and parishioners; pastoral psychology.

Text: A.A.S. 47: 212–17, April 20, 1955.
  TPS (Engl.) 2: 47–51, March 1955.

1956, February 14. *Questo incontro* (address). Lenten message to the pastors and preachers of Rome: priests and charity.

Text: TPS (Engl.) 3: 72–78, Summer 1956.

1956, March 22. *Amadisimos hijos* (address). To the Spanish Pontifical College: priests and holiness of life.

Texts TPS (Engl.) 3: 67–70, Summer 1956.

1956, May 4. *Domine Jesu* (prayer). For the sanctification of the clergy; prayer to be recited by the clergy.

Text: A.A.S. 48: 592, August 1956.
Clergy R. 41: 751, December 1956.

1956, May 31. *Sedes sapientiae* (Apost. Const.). Principles and general statutes for those called to the state of religious perfection.

Text: A.A.S. 48: 354–65, May 1956.
TPS (Engl.) 3: 287–98, Winter 1956.
R. Rel. 16: 88–101, March 1957.

1956, July 17. *O Gesu* (prayer). Prayer for the sanctification of the clergy; to be recited by the laity.

Text: *Priest* (Engl.) 12: 721, September 1956.
A.A.S. (Ital.) 48: 593, August 1956.

1956, September 14. *Di gran cuore* (address). To the Sixth National Congress of the Italian clergy: the preaching of Christ, the priest, and the Church.

Ital. Text: A.A.S. 48: 699–711, October 1956.
Engl. Text: TPS 3: 381–92, Spring 1957.

1957, February 9. *Signor nostro* (prayer). Indulgenced prayer for religious vocations.

Ital. Text: A.A.S. 49: 100, February 1957.

Engl. Text: *Ave* 85: 28, March 30, 1957.
  TPS 4: 28–29, Summer 1957.
  R. Rel. 16: 165, May 1957.

1957, March 5. *Vi diamo* (address). Lenten address to Roman preachers: on religious conditions, immoral literature, lack of vocations in Rome; good and evil in the world; priests; preaching; parable of the sower.

Ital. Text: *A.A.S.* 49: 208–15, April 1957.
Engl. Text: *Cath. Mind* 55: 454–61, October 1957.
  TPS 4: 69–75, Summer 1957.

1957, June 14. *Andísimos hijos* (address). The Ecclesiastical Center of Barcelona: special preparation for young priests.

Engl. Text: *TPS* 4: 185–87 (no. 2, 1957).

1957, September 5. *C'est une grande joie* (address). To a group of French minor seminarians: pilgrims in Rome; Church's value of the priesthood; study; value of minor seminaries.

French Text: *A.A.S.* 49: 845–49, October 1957.
Engl. Text: *A.E.R.* 137: 347–51, November 1957.
  TPS 6: 101–04, Winter 1960.

1957, November 6. *Signore Gesù* (prayer). For vocations to the priesthood.

Ital. Text: *A.A.S.* 49: 1046–47, December 1957.
Engl. Text: *TPS* 4: 392, Spring 1958.

1958, October 19. *Sull' esempio* (address). Prepared for delivery to the seminary of Apulia: on perfection, self-discipline, spiritual strength; the priesthood.

Engl. Text: *Furrow* 10: 189–99, March 1959.

John XXIII (1958–1963)

A Seminarian's Prayer

"O Holy Virgin, Our Lady of Trust, kind and loving Mother of Seminarians throughout the world, your presence once brought joy to the first apostles of the Gospel as they waited tensely and eagerly in the Cenacle for the coming of the Divine Spirit. Look down upon us now, as we stir with the same eager longing for grace and for a priestly zeal that will be holy and bring holiness to others.

Just as you have been our morning star, so always remain the serene joy of our vocation, the safeguard of our purity, the flame of our good work in the service of Jesus and of the souls redeemed by His Blood and of His Church, which suffers at times but always remains glorious and unbowed.

What joy it brings each of us and all of us together, the seminarians of the whole world, to repeat: 'Opus tuum nos, O Maria.' What a sense of exultation always, always to be able to add, at every turn in our lives: we are not afraid of anything, O Mary, for you are and will be our trust, our Mother, 'in aevum et aeternum.'"
(John XXIII, April 7, 1961, TPS 7: 165, 1961)

1958, November 30. *Le espressioni* (address). Exhortation to priests: a spotless life; weakness, humility; zeal in study; steadfast in sacrifice.

Ital. Text: A.A.S. 50: 1012–17, December 1958.
    TPS 6: 96–100, Winter 1960.

1959, February 6. *La familiarita* (letter). To the bishops of Italy: an unfinished letter of Pius XI on seminaries, bishops, the papacy, etc.

Ital. Text: A.A.S. 51: 129–35, March 1959.
    TPS 5: 407–13, Fall 1959.

1959, May 12. *Il Nostro Cuore* (address). To the Apostolic Union of the Clergy: exhortation on the priesthood; example of St. John Vianney.

Ital. Text: A.A.S. 51: 196–202, April 1959.
Engl. Text: *Sursum Corda* 5: 386–92, September 1959.
    TPS 5: 305–9, Summer 1959.

1959, April 21. *A quarantcinque* (message). St. Pius X as example for priests.

Ital. Text: A.A.S. 51: 375–81, May 1959.
Engl. Text: *Cath. Mind* 57: 459–66, October 1959.
    TPS 5: 293–99, Summer 1959.

1959, October 11. The North American College in Rome; the church in America.

Text: A.A.S. 51: 770–75, November 1959.
    Cath. Mind 58: 465–69, October 1960.
    TPS 6: 37–42, Winter 1960.

1959, November 22. Address to seminarians: Three virtues for seminarians: purity, charity, strength of character.

Ital. Text: A.A.S. 51: 903–7, December 1959.
Engl. Text: TPS 6: 164–68, Spring 1960.

1959, November 28. *Princeps pastorum* (encyclical).

Text: A.A.S. 51(1959): 833–64, December 1959.
TPS 6: 123–45, Spring 1960.

1960, January 18. To seminarians studying in Rome; personal reminiscences; exhortation to pray and study.

Text: A.A.S. 52: 262–70, April 1960.
Ital. Text: A.A.S. 52: 271–77, April 1960.

1960, November 24. To the clergy of Rome: the splendor of the priest's mission; detachment from the world.

Ital. Text: A.A.S. 52: 967–79, December 1960.
Engl. Text: TPS 7: 10–22, 1961.

1961, April 6. To Italian seminarians; the seminarian in today's world; apostolic activity.

Engl. Text: TPS 7: 160–64, 1961.

1961, April 7. *O Vergine santa*. Seminarian's indulgenced prayer to Our Lady of Confidence.

Ital. Text: A.A.S. 53: 231, April 1961.
Marianum 23: 480, 1961.
OL Dig. 16: 110, September 1961.
OL Dig. 18: 102, September 1963.
TPS 7: 165, 1961.

1961, April 21. To the First National Italian Congress on Vocations to the Priesthood; the role of the clery; seminary formation; shortage of vocations.

Ital. Text: A.A.S. 53: 308–14, June 1961.
Engl. Text: *Emmanuel* 68: 109–13, March 1962.
  TPS 7: 145–51, 1961.

1961, November 10. To the National Federation of Italian Clergy: priests, co-workers of the bishop, must remember their unique dignity and be loyal to the priestly ideal.

Text: *TPS* 8: 23–25, 1962.

1961, November 11. *Aeterna Dei Sapientia* (encyclical). On the fifteenth centennial of the death of Pope St. Leo I: The See of Peter as the center of Christian Unity.

Text: A.A.S. 53: 785–803, December 1961.
  Cath. Mind 60: 51–62, March 1962.
  TPS 8: 7–22, 1962.
  Unitas 13: 265–80. Winter 1961.

1962, May 26. To the First International Congress on Priestly Vocations; true priestly spirit and activity; fostering vocations through personal example.

Text: A.A.S. 54: 450–53, July 1962.
  TPS 8: 192, 1962. Summary.

1962, August 10. Discourse to seminarians on the fifty-eighth anniversary of his ordination; Jesus, the Good Shepherd, as an example to priests; prayers for coming council.

Ital. Text: A.A.S. 54: 581–89, September 1962.
  TPS 8: 188–189, 1962. Summary.

1963, April 11. *Pacem in terris* (encyclical). On establishing universal peace with truth, justice, charity and liberty.

Text: A.A.S. 55: 257–304, April 1963.
Engl. Text: C. *Lawyer* 10: 28–31, Winter 1964.
   Cath. Mind 61: 47–61, September 1963.
      45–63, October 1963.
   TPS 9: 13–48, 1963.

Paul VI (1963–   )

"*Undoubtedly, priests have no special shelter from the repercussions of the crisis of transformation which is upsetting the world today. Like all their brothers in the faith, they, too, experience hours of darkness in their journey toward God. Moreover, they suffer because of the frequently biased way in which certain facts of priestly life are interpreted and unjustly generalized. Therefore, we ask priests to remember that the situation of every Christian, and particularly of every priest, will always be a paradoxical and incomprehensible situation to those who have no faith. Hence the present state of things urges the priest to deepen his faith, to realize even more clearly to whom he belongs, with what powers he is invested, with what mission he is charged. Beloved sons and brothers, we ask our Lord to make us able and worthy to give you some light, some consolation.*

To all priests, then, we say: Never doubt the nature of your ministerial priesthood, for it is not a commonplace office or service to be exercised for the ecclesial community, but a service which participates in a very special manner, through the sacrament of Orders and with an indelible character, in the power of the priesthood of Christ." *(Paul VI, message to priests, June 30, 1968)*

1963, June 24. To the clergy of Rome; the Pope as Bishop of Rome; religious needs of the city; responsibility of the clergy.

Text: *TPS* 9: 87–88, 1963. Excerpts.

1963, June 27. Address to major and minor seminarians of the Diocese of Rome.

Text: *TPS* 9: 108, 1963. Excerpts.

1963, October 12. To priests of the German-Hungarian College in Rome; to be a priest means to be a servant.

Text: *Emmanuel* 70: 5, January 1964. Engl. excerpts.

1964, September 14. Address at the opening of the third session of Vatican Council II; role of episcopacy.

Text: *TPS* 10: 106–15, Winter 1965.

1964, November 21. *Post duos menses*. On the conclusion of the third session of the Second Vatican Council; Mother of the Church.

Engl. Text: *Cath. Mind* 63: 55–64, January 1965.
  Soc. Just. 58: 106–11, June 1965.
  TPS 10: 131–41, Winter 1965.

1964, December 3. This visit; to representatives of non-Christian religions, on the occasion of the International Eucharistic Congress in Bombay.

Text: *A.A.S.* 57: 130–33, February 27, 1965.
  TPS 10: 154–5, Winter 1965.

1965, March 1. *Non possiamo tacere*. To pastors and Lenten preachers of Rome.

Ital. Text: A.A.S. 57: 325–30, April 30, 1965.
Engl. Text: TPS 10: 228–33, 1965.

1966, February 17. *Paenitemini* (Apost. Const.). The excellence of the virtue of penance as a means of perfection, new fast and abstinence laws established.

Text: A.A.S. 58: 177–98, March 31, 1966.
Jurist 26: 246–64, April 1966.
TPS 11: 362–71, 1966.

1966, February 21. To pastors and lenten preachers of Rome; aggiornamento in the Church depends largely upon priests.

Ital. Text: A.A.S. 58: 225–29, March 31, 1966.
Engl. Text: Soc. Just. 59: 89–91, June 1966.

1966, June 15. *De episcoporum Muneribus* (motu proprio). Bishops' power to dispense from ecclesiastical laws has been enlarged.

Text: A.A.S. 58: 467–72, July 30, 1966.
Engl. Text: Cath. Mind 64: 60–64, October 1966.
Jurist 26: 485–92, October 1966.

1966, July 3. Homily in the Vatican at the ordination to the sacred priesthood of seventy deacons for the Church in Latin America.

Ital. Text: A.A.S. 58: 635–39, September 30, 1966.
Engl. Text: TPS 11:253–58, Summer 1966.

1966, September 9. To participants in the sixteenth Italian Study Week on pastoral updating; parish priests and the spirit of renewal.

Engl. Text: TPS 12: 19–22, 1967.

1967, January 25. To the graduating class of the Pontificio Collegio Beda; the meaning of the sacrament of orders.

Engl. Text: A.A.S. 59: 147–49, February 28, 1967.

1967, March 26. *Populorum progressio* (encyclical). On the development of people.

Text: A.A.S. 58: 257–99, April 15, 1967.
TPS 12: 144–72, 1967.
US Cath. 34: 21–40, August 1968.

1968, February 26. Address to priests and lenten preachers of Rome on the problems of priestly ministry.

Text: A.A.S. 60: 214–19, May 15, 1968.
TPS 13: 113–17, November 2, 1968.

1968, June 30. Motu proprio. The Pope's message to priests on the greatness of their priesthood.

Text: A.A.S. 60: 377–81, July 29, 1968.
Chr. World 13: 388–92, November 5, 1968.

1969, February 17. Address to the lenten preachers of Rome.

Ital. Text: A.A.S. 61: 187–94, March 31, 1969.
TPS 14: 23–29, 1969.
Cath. Mind 67: 54–59, May 1969.

1969, March 21. Address to a group of newly ordained priests.

Engl. Text: OR no. 14 (53), p. 2, April 3, 1969.

1969, March 27. Allocution to the Commission for the Fundamental Principles of Training for the Priesthood.

Text: A.A.S. 61: 253–56, April 30, 1969.

1970, February 9. Address to parish priests and lenten preachers in Rome.
Text: A.A.S. 62: 165–70, March 31, 1970.
OR (Engl.) no. 8 (99), pp. 6–7, February 19, 1970.
TPS 15: 64–69, no. 1, 1970.

1970, May 17. Homily during the ordination of 278 priests in celebration of the fiftieth anniversary of the ordination of the Pope.
Text: OR (Engl.) no. 22, (113), p. 1, May 28, 1970.
TPS 15: 141–45 (no. 2, 1970).

1970, May 18. Address to cardinals after congratulations on fiftieth anniversary.
Text: A.A.S. 62: 448–52, July 30, 1970.
TPS 15: 129–33 (no. 2, 1970).
ORS (Engl.) no. 22 (113), pp. 6–7, May 28, 1970.

1970, May 30. Address to Polish priests once in concentration camps who were on pilgrimage to Rome.
Engl. Text: OR no. 24 (115), p. 1f., June 11, 1970.

1970, June 25. Address to a group of priests from the Diocese of Brescia urging them to respect tradition.
Engl. Text: OR no. 28 (119), p. 3f., July 9, 1970.

1970, September 30. Address to Apostolic Union of the Clergy meeting in Rome.
Fr. Text: Doc. Cath. 67: 960, November 1, 1970.

1970, November 28. Address to the Assembly of Bishops in Manila.

Text: *Cath Mind* 69: 60–64, February 1971.
      OR (Engl.) no. 49 (140), pp. 6–7, December 3, 1970.

1970, November 30. Address to the clergy after Mass in St. Mary's Cathedral, Sydney.

Engl. Text: *OR* no. 50 (141), p. 19, December 10, 1970.

1970, December 1. Address delivered to joint episcopal conferences of Australia and Oceania in crypt of St. Mary's Cathedral, Sydney, Australia.

Text: *TPS* 15: 386–90, 1971.

1970, December 2. Address to elderly priests, Sydney, Australia.

Text: *OR* (Engl.) no. 51 (142), p. 2, December 17, 1970.
      TPS 15: 390–92, 1971.

1971, February 20. Address to Roman clergy and lenten preachers.

Text: *OR* (Engl.) no. 9 (153), pp. 6–7, March 4, 1971.
      TPS 16: 57–62 (no. 1, 1971).

1971, March 25. Address to presidents and delegates of the European Episcopal Conference Meeting in Rome.

Text: *A.A.S.* 63: 291–92, April 30, 1971.
      OR (Engl.) no. 14 (158), p. 9, April 8, 1971.

1971, March 31. Address to a group of newly ordained priests from Beda College in Rome.

Text: *OR* (Engl.) no. 14 (158), p. 3, April 8, 1971.

1971, April 4. Address to newly ordained priests of the Salesian Univ. of Rome.

The Priesthood in Papal Documents

Text: OR (Engl.) no. 15 (159), p. 8, April 15, 1971.

1971, June 12. Address to students and newly ordained priests from ecclesiastical colleges in Rome.

Text: OR (Engl.) no. 25 (169), p. 4f., June 29, 1971.
TPS 16: 100–3, 1971.

1971, September 8. Address to priests at National Meeting of Diocesan Ecclesiastical Counselors.

Text: OR (Engl.) no. 39 (183), p. 3, September 30, 1971.

1971, October 6. Address explaining the function of the hierarchy during the Third Synod of Bishops.

Text: OR (Engl.) no. 41 (185), p. 1, October 14, 1971.
TPS 16: 215–17, 1971.

1971, October 13. Address to a general audience about priesthood.

Text: OR (Engl.) no. 42 (186), pp. 2–3, October 21, 1971.
TPS 16: 211–14, 1971.

1971, October 17. Homily during beatification of Father Maximilian Kolbe, O.F.M.

Text: OR (Engl.) no. 43 (187), pp. 8–9, October 28, 1971.
TPS 16: 238–43, 1971.

1971, October 17. Address in St. Peter's Square after beatification of Fr. Kolbe, O.F.M.

Text: OR (Engl.) no. 42 (186), October 21, 1971.

1971, November 6. Address at conclusion of Third International Synod of Bishops (September 30–November 6, 1971).

Text: OR (Engl.) no. 46 (190), pp. 8–9, November 18, 1971.
　　　A.A.S. 63: 831–37, November 30, 1971.
　　　Cath. Mind 70: 60–64, January 1972.
　　　T.P.S. 16: 198–204, 1971.

6 The Pope and Vatican Council II

"Priests, prudent cooperators with the episcopal order as well as its aids and instruments, are called to serve the people of God. They constitute one priesthood with their bishop, although that priesthood is comprised of different functions. Associated with their bishop in a spirit of trust and generosity, priests make him present in a certain sense in the individual local congregations of the faithful, and take upon themselves, as far as they are able, his duties and concerns, discharging them with daily care. As they sanctify and govern under the bishop's authority that part of the Lord's flock entrusted to them, they make the universal Church visible in their locality and lend powerful assistance to the upbuilding of the whole body of Christ (cf. Eph. 4:12). Intent always upon the welfare of God's children, they must strive to lend their effort to the pastoral work of the whole diocese, and even of the entire church."
Vatican II, Dogmatic Constitution on the Church, 28)

FATHERS OF VATICAN COUNCIL II (1962–1965)

1963, December 4. *Sacrosanctum Concilium.* Constitution on the Sacred Liturgy.

Text: A.A.S. 56: 97–144, February 15, 1964.
Jurist 24: 1–43, January 1964.
R. Rel. 23: 561–91, September 1964.
TPS 9: 316–38, 1964.

1964, November 21. *Lumen Gentium* Dogmatic Constitution on the Church.

Text: A.A.S. 57: 5–71, January 30, 1965.
Engl: A.E.R. 152: 33–57, January 1965.
115–39, February 1965.
R. Rel. 24: 665–734, Summer 1965.
Soc. Just. 58: 116–53, June 1965.

1965, October 28. *Christus Dominus.* Decree concerning the pastoral office of Bishops in the Church.

Text: A.A.S. 58: 673–701, October 8, 1966.
Engl. Text: *Jurist* 26: 4–34, January 1966.
Priest 21: 5A–27A, December 1965.

1965, October 28. *Optatam Totius.* Decree on Priestly Training.

Text: A.A.S. 58: 713–27, October 8, 1966.
Engl. Text: *Jurist* 26: 129–48, April, 1966.
Priest 21: 1B–12B, December 1965.
TPS 11: 17–30, Winter 1966.

1965, December 7. *Gaudium et Spes*. Pastoral Constitution on the Church in the Modern World.

Text: A.A.S. 58: 1025–1120, December 7, 1966.
Engl. Text: *Jurist* 26: 426–53, October 1966.
    Priest 22: 1A–84A, February 1966.
    TPS 11: 259–323, Summer, 1966.

1965, December 7. *Presbyterorum Ordinis*. Decree on the Ministry and Life of Priests.

Text: A.A.S. 58: 991–1024, November 30, 1966.
    Priest 22: 1C–27C, February 1966.
    TPS 11: 442–68, 1966.

AMERICAN BISHOPS

"Let us be even more candid. The ministry which we as bishops share with our brother-priests becomes bearable and fruitful in the degree of our mutual fidelity, our faithfulness to priests, their loyalty to us. If it be true, as it is, that because we are men we know the burdens of priests, it is also true that because they are priests they know the special burdens which trouble us. In times of greatest stress, next only to the presence of the Paraclete, it is the solidarity of priests, compactly closed around us, their understanding, their unselfish devotion, their persevering work, the laughter and the tears they and we share, which blend with all the resources of nature and grace, to enable us the better to perform every priestly function that Christ committed to the college of His apostles in communion with Peter. This priestly office we share with all the priests in union with us." (NCCB, The Church in Our Day, *January, 21, 1968, pp. 40–41)*

1968, January 21 NCCB. *The Church in Our Day: A collective Pastoral of the American Hierarchy on the Mystery of the Church.* Washington, D.C.: USCC, 1968.

THE THIRD SYNOD OF BISHOPS

"By the laying on of hands there is communicated a gift of the Holy Spirit which cannot be lost (cf. 2 Tim. 1:6). This reality configures the ordained minister to Christ the Priest, consecrates him (cf. P.O. 2) and makes him a sharer in Christ's mission under its two aspects of authority and service.

That authority does not belong to the minister as his own: it is a manifestation of the 'exousia' (i.e. the power) of the Lord, by which the priest is an ambassador of Christ in the eschatological work of reconciliation (cf. 2 Cor. 5:18–20). He also assists the conversion of human freedom to God for the building up of the Christian community." (The Ministerial Priesthood, *pt. 1, 5, Synod of Bishops, 1971)*

1971, November 5. *The Ministerial Priesthood.* Synodal document.

Text: OR (Engl.) no. 50 (194), pp. 1–4, December 16, 1971.
Cath. Mind 70: 33–51, March 1972.

Reprint. *Priests of the Sacred Heart.* Hales Corner, Wis., 1972, 24pp.

Reprint. NCCB. Synod of Bishops. *The Ministerial Priesthood; Justice in the World.* USCC, 1972, 52pp.

Epilogue

"... *The priest is no longer for himself, he is for the ministry of Christ's Mystical Body. He is a servant, an instrument of the Word and of grace. The proclamation of the Gospel, the celebration of the Eucharist, the remission of sins, the exercise of pastoral activity, the life of faith and worship, and the radiation of charity and holiness are his duty, a duty that reaches the point of self-sacrifice, of the cross, as for Jesus. It is a very heavy burden. But Jesus bears it with his chosen one and makes him feel the truth of his words: 'my yoke is easy and my burden light.' (Mt. 11:30). For, as Saint Augustine teaches us, 'my weight is my love' (Conf. 13:9). When love of Christ becomes the single supreme principle of the life of a priest, it makes all easy, all possible, all happy..."* (Address at the ordination of Asiatic priests at Luneta Park, Manila, November 28, 1970. OR no. 50 [141], p. 1, December 10, 1970)

A Prayer for Vocations to the Priesthood

"Lord Jesus, Supreme Priest and Universal Pastor, Who taught us to pray, saying "Pray therefore the Lord of the harvest to send forth laborers into his harvest" (Matt. 9, 38), kindly hear our supplications and raise up many generous souls who, animated by Your example and sustained by Your grace, will aspire to be the ministers and perpetuators of Your true and only priesthood.

Grant that the snares and calumnies of the evil foe, supported by the indifferent and materialistic spirit of the century, will not dim among the faithful that lofty splendor and that profound esteem due to the mission of those who, without being of the world, live in the world to be dispensers of the divine mysteries.

Grant that religious instruction, sincere piety, purity of life, and respect for the highest ideals will always continue to be promoted in youth so that good vocations may be prepared. May they be supported by a Christian family which will never cease to be the nursery of unspoiled and fervent souls and which will ever remain conscious of the honor of giving some of its abundant offspring to God.

Grant that Your Church itself in all parts of the world will not lack the necessary means to receive, promote, form, and bring to maturity the good vocations which are offered it.

And in order that all this may be realized, O Jesus, Who art most concerned with the welfare and salvation of all, grant that the irresistible power of Your grace will *not cease to descend from heaven until it has penetrated many spirits: first called silently, then responding generously and finally persevering in Your holy service.*

Are You not afflicted, O Lord, at seeing such multitudes as flocks without a shepherd, without anyone to nourish them with the bread of Your words, without anyone to bring them the water of Your grace, in danger of being at the mercy of the rapacious wolves who constantly lie in wait for them? Do You not suffer at seeing so many fields untouched by the blade of the plow, where thistles and thorns grow without anyone to fight for ground against them? Are You not pained at seeing Your gardens, once blossoming and green, about to become yellow and untended? Will You allow such abundant harvests, now mature, to shed their grain and be lost for want of arms to gather them?

O Mother Mary, most pure, from whose compassionate hands we received the most holy of all priests; O Glorious Patriarch St. Joseph, perfect example of response to God's call; O all you priests, saints who form a beloved choir around the Lamb of God in heaven: obtain for us many and good vocations so that the flocks of the Lord, supported and guided by vigilant pastors, will be able to enter the most sweet pastures of eternal happiness. Amen." (Pius XII, November 6, 1957, TPS *4: 392, 1958)*

Index of Authors

Abbott, W. M., 48
Ahern, P. H., 35
Alphonsus de Liguori, St., 42
Anciaux, P., 48
Aradi, Z., 34, 37
Armitage, A., 33
Augustine, St., 26
Audet, J., 48
Bacuez, L., 42
Barrett, E. B., 32
Barry, C. J., 36
Bastian, R., 48
Bazin, R., 20
Beahn, J. E., 26
Belair, R., 20
Benson, A. C., 32
Bernanos, G., 20
Bernard, St., 26
Betz, E., 29, 32, 33
Bishop, J., 33
Biskupek, A., 42
Blomjous, J., 48
Blount, M., 37
Bocquet, M., 36
Bolton, I., 38
Bonn, J., 34
Bordeaux, H., 20
Bordelon, M., 48
Borelli, M., 32
Boresky, T., 28
Bourke, V. J., 26
Boylan, M. E., 42
Boyle, G., 39
Boyton, N., 27
Brady, L., 20

Bregy, K., 27
Broderick, F., 38
Brodrick, A. H., 32
Brodrick, J., 26, 29
Broucher, J., 33
Brown, R., 48
Bruneau, J., 42, 54
Buehrle, M., 36, 39
Bunnik, R., 48
Burton, K., 28, 29, 33, 34, 35, 39
Caldwell, T., 20
Caraman, P., 36
Carey, K., 32
Carmignano, A., 28
Carroll, M., 29
Carrouges, M., 32
Cather, W., 20
Centre de Pastorale Liturgique, 42
Cesbron, G., 20
Charue, A. M., 42
Chesterton, G. K., 20, 29
Cicognani, A., 42
Ciszek, W., 33
Clancy, J., 37
Clausen, S., 26
Cloupeau, J., 27
Coccioli, C., 20
Cohausz, O., 42
Colaianni, J., 48
Cole, M., 34
Collins, W., 33
Congar, Y., 48
Congregation for Catholic Education, 48
Connell, F. J., 42

Index of Authors

Cooper, E., 20
Corbishley, T., 35
Courtois, G., 42
Crawley-Boevey, M., 42
Cristiani, L., 28
Cronin, A. J., 20
Cronin, V., 38
Crosbie, R., 33
Cross, C., 38
Cunningham, M., 20
Curley, M., 28
Curtayne, A., 29
Cushing, R., 42
Cutler, J., 33
Dal-Gal, H., 29
Daniel-Rops, H., 28, 30
D'Arcy, P., 48
De LaBedoyere, M., 33
De Terra, H., 39
Dever, J., 20, 33
Devlin, C., 29
DeWohl, L., 20
Dillenschneider, C., 42, 48
Doherty, E. J., 27
Dominian, H., 32
Donahue, G., 42
Dorcy, M. J., 26
Doty, W., 21
Dougherty, J., 42
Dudley, O. F., 21
Duggan, A., 29
Dupeyrat, A., 33
Durkin, J., 38
Eder, K., 42
Edwards, E., 21
Ellis, J. T., 34, 39, 48
Englebert O., 21, 38
Engleman, J., 42
Fabian, B., 36
Faherty, W., 21
Farrow, J., 33
Father X., 33
Fenton, J., 43
Ferguson, C., 39

Fichter, J., 48
Fischer, M., 29
Foley, A., 34
Forrest, M., 37
Fourrey, R., 29
Fransen, P., 48
Furlan, W., 37
Gallagher, J. P., 34
Gannon, D., 37
Gannon, M., 39
Gannon, R., 39
Gardiner, H. C., 27
Garesche, E., 43
Garrigou-Lagrange, R., 43
Gerard, J., 34
Gheon, H., 27, 28, 30
Gibbons, J., 41, 43
Ginder, R., 37
Giordani, I., 28, 29
Girandola, A., 34
Gironella, J. M., 21
Godden, R., 21
Goebel, B., 43
Goldman, G., 34
Goudge, E., 21
Grabman, M., 29
Grant, D. F., 33, 39
Greeley, A., 48, 49
Greene, G., 21
Greene, R., 34
Grieco, R., 29
Guareschi, G., 21
Gumbley, W., 28
Gwynn, D. R., 32, 39
Habig, M. A., 26
Halecki, O., 37
Halevy, L., 21
Hallack, C., 21
Hallett, P. H., 27
Harland, H., 21
Hatch, A., 37
Hayne, D., 34
Healy, K., 54
Hebert, A. J., 49

Index of Authors

Heckler, V., 49
Hefer, J., 28
Hermand, P., 49
Heston, E., 43
Hildebrand, P. von, 49
Hilkert, R., 33
Holden, V. F., 34
Holland, C., 43
Hollis, C., 28
Holy Cross Quarterly, 32
Homan, H. W., 28
Horgan, P., 21
Huber, G., 35
Hudson, J. W., 21
Hunermann, W., 29
Jacks, L. V., 33
Jamison, J. K., 32
Janney, R., 21
Janssen, J., 43
Joahandeau, M., 29
John XXIII, Pope, 35, 56-57, 64-68
John Chrysostom, St., 43
John Eudes, St., 43
Jungmann, J., 49
Kane, G. L., 35, 43
Karrer, O., 49
Kassiepe, M., 43
Kaye-Smith, S., 22
Keatinge, J., 43
Keller, J., 35, 43
Kelley, F. C., 35, 43
Keneally, T., 22
Kennedy, E., 48, 49
Kerby, W. J., 43
Kerrison, R., 39
Kiefer, W., 35
Kirlin, J. L., 43
Klaver, R., 43
Knox, R. A., 35, 43
Kuhn, A., 27
La Farge, J., 35
Lane, R., 32
Lash, N., 49
Lattin, H., 39

Lauro, J., 35
Leckie, R., 22
Leclercq, J., 49
Lecuyer, J., 43
Ledit, J., 33
Leen, E., 43
Leow, J., 35
Lepp, I., 35
Leslie, S., 34, 36
Lewis, D. B. W., 29
Lewis, M., 22
Lindop, A., 22
Liturgical Conference, 43-44
Lomask, M., 26, 28
Lord, D., 35
Lovasik, L., 44
Loyola University Study, 49
Luddy, A. J. O., 28
MacEoin, G., 36
Machlem, M., 27
MacManus, F., 27
MacNeill, E., 28
Madden, W. J., 44
Magaret, H., 26, 36
Maguire, W., 36
Mahoney, E. J., 44
Mannin, E., 22
Manning, H. E., 44
Manzoni, A., 22
Marcetteau, B., 44
Maritain, J., 29
Maritain, R., 29
Marmion, C., 44
Marshall, B., 22
Martin Descalzo, J., 36
Martindale, C. C., 26, 27
Martini, T., 38
Mary Elanore, M., 28
Mast, D., Sr., 38
Masure, E., 44
Mauriac, F., 22
Maynard, T., 29, 30, 38
McGoey, J., 35, 44, 49
McGratty, A., 27

Pattee, R., 39
Paul VI, Pope, 13-14, 46-47, 50, 69-76, 83
Pellegrino, M., 50
Perrin, H., 37
Peters, W., 32
Peyton, P., 38
Pezeril, D., 22, 30
Pfau, R., 37
Pfliegler, M., 44
Phelan, M., 44
Pierre, A., 37
Pies, O., 35
Pittini, R., 37
Pius X, Pope, St., 51, 54
Pius XI, Pope, 51-52, 54
Pius XII, Pope, 54-56, 60-63, 85-86
Plassman, T., 44
Poage, G., 44
Pohlschneider, J., 44
Power, C., 22
Powers, J. F., 22
Prescott, H. F. M., 22
Purcell, M., 27, 28, 30
Queffelec, H., 22
Rahner, K., 50
Ratzinger, J., 50
Raven, C., 39
Raymond, A., 33
Raymond, M., 26, 38
Read, P., 22
Reinhold, H. A., 37
Repplier, A., 36
Retif, L., 44, 50
Reynolds, E. E., 27, 32
Reynolds, Q., 28
Ricciotti, G., 29
Richardson, M., 39
Rigney, H., 38
Rihn, R., 50
Robinson, H. M., 22
Rogers, P., 36
Romaniello, J., 22, 38
Romb, A. W., 50

McLaverty, M., 22
Meadows, D., 36
Melville, A., 33
Mercier, D. J., 36
Merton, T., 36
Michonneau, G., 36
Middleton, J., 44
Mohler, J., 49
Mojica, J. F., 36
Montini, G., 13-14, 46-47, 50, 69-76, 83
Moore, E., 36
Morris, B., 54
Moseley, D. H., 29
Moynihan, J., 34
Muller, M., 27
Mulvey, T., 36
Murphy, E., 36
Murphy, F. X., 35
Murray, J. C., 39
Murrett, J., 37
Mydans, S., 22
Myers, R., 36, 44
Nash, R., 44
Navagh, J. J., 44
National Conference of Catholic Bishops, 49, 80
National Opinion Research Center, 49
Newcomb, C., 32, 34, 36
Noppell, C., 44
Nouwen, H. J., 49
Novak, M., 22
O'Brien, I., 26
O'Brien, J., 44
O'Connell, D. P., 38
O'Connor, E., 22
O'Donnell, T., 44
O'Faolain, S., 36
O'Meara, J. J., 26
O'Neill, D., 50
Oursler, F., 34
Palmer, G., 34, 37
Parente, P. P., 37

Index of Authors

Roos, A., 27
Rope, H. E. G., 32
Roy, G. C., 22
Royer, F., 27, 37
Russell, S., 38
Ryan, T., 38
Sampson, F., 38
Santen, H., 32
Sargent, D., 27, 28, 34, 39
Schaefer, W., 44
Schauinger, J. H., 32, 34
Schelke, K., 50
Schillebeeckx, E., 50
Schofield, W., 23
Schrijvers, J., 45
Sellmair, J., 45
Shaw, J. G., 37
Shaw, S., 45
Sheehan, P., 23
Sheehy, M. S., 23
Sheeran, J., 38
Sheppard, L., 27, 35
Simon, M. R., 38
Simonet, A., 50
Sloyan, G., 50
Smyth, B., 38
Spicq, C., 45
Steinmann, J., 28
Stockums, W., 45
Suenens, L., 50
Suhard, E., 45
Suigo, C., 39
Synod of Bishops, III, 1971, 81
Talbot, F., 28
Tardini, D., 37
Tartre, R., 50
Tehan, A., 34
Tennien, M., 39
Thils, G., 50
Thorton, F., 37
Tonne, A., 35
Trappes-Lomax, M., 33
Treat, R., 38
Trese, L., 45
Trevor, M., 35
Trochu, F., 30
Trouncer, M., 30
Tull, C., 33
Urtasun, J., 45
Valtierra, A., 27
Van der Meer, F., 26
Van Kaam, A., 28
Van Zeller, H., 39, 45
Vatican Council II, 50, 77-79
Vaughan, J., 45
Vehenne, H., 37
Waddell, H., 23
Walsh, J. E., 35
Walsh, J. J., 39
Walsh, W. T., 29
Ward, J., 38
Ward, M., 36
Waugh, E., 27
Wayman, D., 37
Weber, R., 39
Werfel, F., 23
West, M., 23
Weston, W., 39
Whealon, John F., 11
White, H. C., 23
Wilham of St. Thierry, 26
Windeatt, M., 28, 30
Winowska, M., 28, 35
Wise, E. V., 23
Woodford, F., 38
Woodgate, M. V., 27
Yeo, M., 26
Yzermans, V., 54
Ziegler, I., 23

Index of Subjects

Abelard, Peter, 23
Alberic, St., 38
Albert, The Great, St., 26
Aloysius Gonzaga, St., 26
Alphonsus Liguori, St., 26
Anchieta, Jose de, 32
Anthony, of Padua, St., 26
Augustine, St., 20, 26
Badin, Stephen, 32
Baraga, Frederic, 32
Barber, Virgil, 32
Barberi, Dominic, 32
Bartolome de Las Casas, 32
Bellarmine, Robert, St., 26
Benedict, St., 20
Benedict XV, Pope, 32
Benson, Robert H., 32
Bernard, St., 26
Berrigan, Daniel, 32
Berrigan, Philip, 32
Bishop, W. Howard, 32
Borgia, Francis, St., 26
Bosco, John, St., 27
Bossuet, Jacques, 32
Breuil, Henri, 32
Brute de Remur, Simon, 38
Bunel, Lucien, 32
Byrne, Patrick J., 32
Cajetan, St., 27
Camara, Helder, 33
Camillus, St., 27
Campion, Edmund, St., 27
Cardijn, Joseph, 33
Carroll, John, 33
Challoner, Richard, 33

Chaminade, William J., 33
Chanel, Peter, St., 27
Chaplains, military
   Crosbie, *March Till*, 33
   Bishop, *Fighting Father Duffy*, 33
   Tonne, *Kapaun*, 35
   Lauro, *Action Priest*, 35
   Maguire, *Captain*, 36
   _____, *Rig for Church*, 36
   Mulvey, *These Are Your*, 36
   Sampson, *Look Out Below*, 38
   _____, *Paratrooper*, 38
   Sheeran, *Confederate*, 38
   Cross, *Soldiers of God*, 38
   Grant, *War Is My Parish*, 39
Chaplains, prison
   Bonn, *Gates of Dannemora*, 34
Cheverus, Jean L. de, 33
Cieplak, John B., 33
Claret, Anthony, St., 27
Claver, Peter, St., 27
Columban, St., 27
Copernicus, Nicholas, 33
Corridan, John M., 33
Coughlin, Charles E., 33
Crawley-Boevey, Mateo, 36
Cushing, Richard, 33
Damien, Father, 33
Dubuis, Claude, 33
Duffy, Francis, 33
England, John, 33
Farmer, Ferdinand, 33
Ferrer, Vincent, St., 27
Fidelis, Father, 39
Fisher, John, St., 27

Index of Subjects

Flaget, Benedict, 34
Flanagan, Edward, 34
Fox, Robert J., 34
Francis de Sales, St., 27
Francis Solanus, St., 27
Francis Xavier, St., 20, 27
Gallitzin, Demetrius, 34
Gasquet, Francis, 34
Gerbert, 39
Gibbons, James, 34
Grignon de Montfort, Louis Mary, St., 28
Healy, James A., 34
Hecker, Isaac T., 34
Hyland, Ambrose R., 34
Ignatius, St., 20, 28
Ireland, John, 34
Isaac Jogues, St., 28
Jerome, St., 28
John XXIII, Pope, 34, 35
John Capistran, St., 28
John Eudes, St., 28
John of the Cross, St., 28
Josaphat, St., 28
Kapaun, Emil J., 35
Keane, John J., 35
Knox, Ronald A., 35
Kolbe, Maximilian, Ven., 28, 35
Lacordaire, Jean B., 35
Lawrence of Brindisi, St., 28
Leisner, Karl, 35
Leo XIII, Pope, 35
Lercaro, Giacomo, 35
Libermann, Francis, Ven., 28
Malachy, St., 28
Manning, Henry E., 36
Marquette, Jacques, 36
Martin of Tours, St., 28
Mathew, Theobald, 36
McShane, Daniel L., 35
Merry Del Val, Rafael, 36
Mindszenty, Josef, 36
Moreau, Basil, 36
Morse, Henry, 36

Muench, Aloisius, 36
Nerinckx, Charles, 36
Neumann, John, Ven., 28
Newman, John H., 36
Noll, John F., 37
O'Connell, William H., 37
O'Hara, Edwin V., 37
Pacelli, Eugenio, 37
Pallotti, Vincenzo, St., 28
Patrick, St., 23, 28
Paul, St., 20, 28, 29
Paul VI, Pope, 37
Paul, James Francis, Fr., 37
Peter, St., 29
Peter Canisius, St., 29
Philip Benizi, St., 29
Philip Neri, St., 29
Pierz, Francis X., 37
Pio, Padre, 37
Pire, Dominic, 37
Pius IX, Pope, 37
Pius X, Pope, St., 29
Pius XI, Pope, 37
Pius XII, Pope, 37
Plunkett, Oliver, St., 29
Price, Thomas F., 37
Pro, Michael, 37
Ricci, Matteo, 38
Richard, Gabriel, 38
Richelieu, Armand J., 38
Robert, St., 38
Ryan, John A., 38
Scalabrini, John, St., 29
Serra, Junipero, 23, 38
Sheil, Bernard J., 38
Sherman, Thomas E., 38
Shields, Thomas E., 38
Southwell, Robert, St., 29
Spaulding, John L., 39
Spellman, Francis, 39
Stephen Harding, St., 38
Stepinac, Aloysius, 39
Stone, James K., 39
Stritch, Samuel, 39

Index of Subjects

Sylvester II, Pope, 39
Teilhard de Chardin, Pierre, 39
Thomas Aquinas, St., 20, 29
Thomas à Becket, St., 22, 29
Tompkins, James, 39
Trese, Leo, 13
Varin, Joseph, 39
Vernard, Theophane, Ven., 29
Verot, Augustin, 39
Veuster, Joseph de, 33

Vianney, John Marie, St., 29, 30
Vincent de Paul, St., 30
Walsh, James A., 39
Walsh, James E., 39
Wattson, Lewis T., 37
Weigel, Gustave, 39
Wiseman, Nicholas P., 39
Wolsey, Thomas, 39
Zahm, John, 39